# DARKNESS THERE BUT SOMETHING MORE

CASSANDRA O'SULLIVAN SACHAR

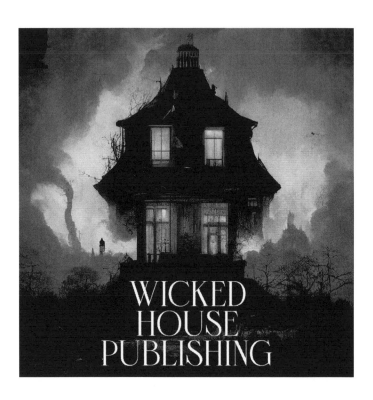

**Darkness There but Something More**
**By Cassandra O'Sullivan Sachar**

**Wicked House Publishing**

Cover design by Christian Bentulan
Interior Formatting by Duncan Ralston

*For Simon*

# PROLOGUE

They enter the path in single file, a curving snake of girls, the sorority pledge mistress at the helm. At midnight in October, only the narrow flashlight beams and glow of the full moon illuminate the way through the blackened forest.

Clad in thin T-shirts and boxer shorts, the pledges tremble and quake. Even the sisters, properly attired in winter coats and hats, feel the chill, but the pledges are quivering gooseflesh. The howling wind whips their hair around their heads and bites their exposed skin.

"Faster," the pledge mistress says over the crunch of the crisp, dead leaves on which they walk. The naked trees stretch out above, their long limbs reaching out to poke or prod. Ice cold, the girls tread over jagged rocks that stub their sneaker-clad toes.

The chatter of her teeth pounds in the girl's head, filling the near silence. Her meager clothes, stiff with grime, reek of body odor—pledges are not allowed to shower during Hell Week. The acrid taste of bile fills the girl's mouth as she trudges on toward whatever horror the pledge mistress has planned.

Numb. She feels numb, both in body and spirit. What is she doing here? Why walk half-naked in the freezing night whe:

she could be curled up in bed in her dorm room under a comforter? All of this misery for the privilege of wearing some stupid Greek letters? All of this stress and drama to belong to the organization of her tormentors?

A tear creeps down her face, its warmth a tiny comfort.

"Stop. We're here." There's a slight smile in the pledge mistress's voice, but all the girl can see in the faint light is a great chasm.

The assistant pledge mistress, the kinder, gentler one, takes over. Clearing her throat, she begins her speech. "This is the Cliff of Life Ritual. Pledges, if you want to belong to the sisterhood, you need to stand here in solidarity, holding hands and leaning on each other for support. You'll get through this, just as all of us sisters have gotten through similar trials. And when you leave, you'll be that much closer to joining our sisterhood. Come."

At first, none of the pledges move, other than the shivers convulsing through their bodies. But then one steps forward, to the cliff's edge, and then the next, until all five girls stand in a row, linked together by their hands.

The sisters watch, rapt with attention, waiting to criticize any signs of weakness. The pledges tremble as they wait, either for relief or more punishment.

Minutes tick by. The girl opens her jaw wide, like a cobra, trying to ensure that her facial muscles still work in the frigidity. She dare not drop her pledge sisters' hands.

Other than the heavy breaths and intermittent mewls and whines of the pledges, only the wind's low moan punctuates the quiet.

A scream cuts through the night.

# CHAPTER 1

Two boxes. That's what it took to pack away the remnants of my career. Two cardboard boxes I pilfered from the copy room.

I remembered arriving at Sainsbury University years earlier with little more than a ton of books and my newly framed Ph.D., nervous as hell but thrilled at securing a tenure-track assistant professor gig in the English Department.

Looking at the blank, beige walls of my office, I felt a frisson of loss. I had seen myself growing old here, had imagined presenting a diploma to my son or daughter as they walked across the stage at graduation.

But that was a pipe dream. I'd never again set foot on Sainsbury's campus, and there would never *be* a son or daughter to present a diploma to, here or anywhere else.

Helen, the secretary, popped her head in my doorway. "I'm so sorry, Marissa. I wish things could have been different." She looked down with watery eyes.

She meant well, but Helen could be a bit much. I held back a sigh and slapped a fake smile on my face. Over the last couple of years, I'd become a pro at acting like everything was okay when I wanted to curl up and cry. "I didn't get fired, Helen! I resigned, and I have a new job. It's time that I moved on."

"I know, but it's just so sad." She dabbed her eyes with a tissue. "And *he's* just strutting around campus with that chippie of his, rubbing it in your face, and now you're leaving!"

Like I needed a reminder. "We're divorced. And I need a fresh start."

I stacked one box on top of the other—I didn't want to take another trip, even if this one would be a struggle.

"Helen, I sincerely want to thank you for your help over the years. Sure, things could have been different. But this is where they are now, and I'm okay. Really."

If I told myself that enough, maybe I'd believe it.

So I left. I walked out that door and off campus for the last time, hoping some of my baggage would remain behind.

---

WHEN I MET David at a faculty happy hour my first year at Sainsbury, I never would have guessed I'd end up marrying him. Or divorcing him, for that matter.

David was a golden boy—actually blond and tan, with ocean blue eyes, looking like he'd just hopped off a surfboard. When I first saw him, I thought back to my Malibu Ken doll. His econ classes always boasted a full roster, with students clamoring to get seats in equal parts for those dashing good looks and David's fame from the semi-regular gigs on CNN.

A pretty big group of faculty members came out that night. I was accustomed to saying no to social gatherings due to my introverted nature, and I was usually so beaten down by the end of a Friday during that hectic first year that all I wanted to do was crash on the couch with Norman, my black cat and constant companion, and a movie. After a full week of lesson planning, teaching, grading, and manning office hours, I had exhausted my brain's capacity to be *on*.

But when Becca, my office suitemate, told me she'd love for me to come hear her husband's band one night, how could I say no? Becca had saved my ass when I couldn't get the copier to work on one of my first days, and she always said hello. I figured I could force myself to be social that particular Friday.

I walked into the dim, cozy bar, nerves fluttering, fifteen minutes late on purpose in hopes Becca would be there first. It was one thing to act friendly, smart, and interesting at work in between classes, but I didn't know what kind of impression I'd make while out at a bar with my colleagues.

Smile frozen on my face, I scanned my surroundings: plush armchairs in the corners, a glossy concrete bar, exposed brick walls. And there was Becca, head thrown back in a laugh, several people I didn't know surrounding her. She had changed her outfit in the last few hours, no longer wearing one of her famous pantsuits. Decked out in a black leather jacket, tight jeans, and knee-high boots, she looked every bit like a rock star's wife. In my work uniform of a navy blazer, sensible shoes, and khakis, I felt more like a librarian than some kind of hip barfly. And not even a *sexy* librarian.

She hadn't seen me yet, and I almost walked right out.

But then we locked eyes, and her face broke into a toothy smile. Gesturing me over, she drew me into a warm embrace. "You came!"

"I told you I would." I should have gotten a drink first—I needed something to do with my hands other than my childish habit of twirling a lock of hair, and her hug caught me off-guard.

"You will *not* be sorry. Brian's band is awesome, and I'm not just saying that because I'm married to the artist." She grabbed the arm of the lanky guy beside her.

He stuck out his hand in a formal gesture which was still far more comfortable for me than the hug. "She's a little biased. But nice to meet you, Marissa! Becca's told me how amazing it is to have another woman, especially a young one, around the office." He gave her a quick peck on the cheek. "I need a drink before the performance. You look like a white wine girl, am I right?"

I laughed, touched that Becca had mentioned me, if a bit embarrassed at how predictable I was. In my attire, I probably didn't look like the kind of person who'd shoot tequila or chug IPAs. "That would be great."

With Brian off to the bar, Becca pointed me in the direction of the others huddled around, standing and in chairs. A few faces, all in their thirties or forties, looked familiar, but I hadn't talked to any of them before. "I don't know if any of you have met each other. This is Marissa Owens, our new hire in the English Department."

I didn't mind at all that Becca claimed me, as it made me feel like I belonged. I waved my hand in an awkward half-arc movement. "Hi. Nice to meet all of you."

It wasn't, not really—my anxiety flared up at the thought that I'd have to seem cool in front of all of these relaxed-looking, bar-going people—but I knew that I was supposed to at least *act* like a normal human.

David was the first to say something. "I know you! Aren't you the Poe scholar? I read your piece in *The Washington Post*."

My cheeks flamed, and I hoped the murky lighting didn't give me away. Luckily, Brian arrived with my drink right at that moment, so I took a quick swallow. "My biggest claim to fame on a very short list of publications," I said. "I'm pretty sure that's why I was hired."

He clinked my glass with his pint of beer. "Cheers to your success, and welcome to Sainsbury. I'm David Hanlon.

Economics. Not as cool as Poe, but it pays the bills." He flashed a dazzling smile—perfectly straight, white teeth—and my stomach flipped.

I stayed and listened to Brian's band, which was surprisingly good, just the right balance of blues and rock, and hung out with these other professors who exuded effortless charisma. As I laughed and talked and drank maybe one more glass of wine than I should have, I finally felt at ease and allowed myself to enjoy the evening.

After what happened during college, I had developed a mistrust of handsome men, but David seemed different. His looks weren't even what captivated me—it was his charm, his wit. But his appearance didn't hurt the equation. When David drew me in with that blue-eyed gaze, it was like I was the only woman in the room.

AS DISSIMILAR AS we were on the surface, we clicked. He told me he'd never dated someone smarter than him, and he liked my nerdiness, how I could bust out with a line from a number of novels without batting an eye or resorting to Google. He said he admired my work ethic and the focus I gave to my career.

I'd always been a bit of a loner and hadn't dated that much, but I loved how being part of a couple made me feel. There I was on the arm of David Hanlon, invited to parties at the fancy houses of senior faculty members, elected to committees that would count as service when it was time to go up for tenure and promotion. Though I'd never been one of the popular girls, David was my ticket into a different world. A social butterfly who put me at ease in group functions, he was sweet and attentive one-on-one, as well. I had never felt so special or cherished.

*We loved with a love that was more than love.* Well, maybe Poe's narrator and Annabel Lee had something greater, but David and I were engaged within a year.

When the wedding prep started and I begged for a small event, he had a tough time understanding. Born to a large family on an expansive Connecticut estate, he didn't *get* my own lack of people, how I had only a few relations and a handful of friends from grad school I wanted to invite. But we loved each other, so we compromised. We appeased his parents with a party on their terms, and we celebrated our legal wedding, just the two of us, on a beach in Jamaica.

We had some really good times over the years. He was there for me when my biography of Poe, the work I had toiled over for years, got rejected by every major publisher as well as the indie ones. A shinier, glossier, contact lens-wearing version of myself with keratin-straightened hair, laser-smoothed legs, and whitened teeth, I was there on his arm for dinners and conferences where he was honored or asked to be the keynote speaker. He was the sun, and I dwelt in the shadows. But I was happy there, ecstatic to be in his orbit.

Despite the disappointment of my book, I managed to publish several piecemeal articles from it, so I still earned tenure and promotion from assistant to associate professor. After that major hassle, we started trying to expand our family. David was desperate to carry on the Hanlon name, especially since I hadn't taken his—I explained that I wanted to keep my maiden name for scholarship reasons.

After a year of "let's try and see what happens," we got more serious. By that time, I was almost thirty-seven and in the geriatric pregnancy zone. First, we tracked my ovulation. Eventually, we saw a fertility specialist. I self-injected the shots and tried to manage my moodiness.

The thing is, I had never really wanted a baby. I hadn't thought much about it. With my own less-than-idyllic childhood, becoming a parent wasn't ever a goal, but David was so excited that I ended up catching baby fever, too. Each month, getting my period seemed like a failure of my womanhood, as if my body couldn't perform its one job.

I grew anxious, just as I did when I was deep in research. Those dots of blood in my underwear felt like a rejection letter from a publisher in my inbox. I hoped and prayed for an acceptance, in this case a pregnancy, and then it was the biggest letdown.

Every. Single. Time.

David was a champ, helping with the needles, rubbing my feet, and pampering me. And I saw his heart break each time I told him we weren't pregnant, month after month.

So we got more aggressive with the treatments. I canceled a bunch of classes for all the appointments, but I had sick days saved up from my many years of loyal service, and at least I was already tenured by then, so I was under less scrutiny. The fertility drugs made it hard to concentrate on grading essays sometimes, and I even had a student complaint that went all the way to the dean's office.

I had thought all those sacrifices would pay off when I became a mother. In those baby-hungry years, I would walk past the diaper aisle in the grocery store and pick up packages, looking at the sizes. I found myself studying jars of baby food to memorize how old my baby would need to be for the different stages. And the clothes—the footie pajamas, the tiny overalls. Every now and then, I'd give in and buy something, hiding it in the closet or a drawer.

Someday, I imagined bringing out these treasures for my own little person.

But that day never came. It *almost* did. I wasn't that surprised when, after a positive pregnancy test, I miscarried within the first trimester. We didn't want to get our hopes up the second time, the third, or even the fourth, but things were going so well during my fifth pregnancy.

Until they weren't, and I went home without a baby but with a jagged scar bisecting my middle.

After everything happened, all the awful bits I tried to sweep under the rug, David and I were too sad and depleted to talk about it much. Even the marriage counselor we went to offered little advice on moving forward.

I was the one who left. It was David's money, mainly, that bought the house—I hadn't ended up going for full professor after my book failed, and my teaching evals had slipped. It didn't seem right for me to stay and wait for *him* to move out.

David wasn't a bad guy, but we didn't harmonize anymore. The magic we once shared had drained away, and we became two people who cohabitated and little else. When he finally served me with the divorce papers, all I felt was a dull ache. I'd already experienced rock bottom.

So I signed, contacted a lawyer, and moved the rest of my stuff out of the house. I threw myself back into my work. I was uninspired to complete any significant scholarship, but I wanted to improve my teaching.

I had essentially stopped socializing during those years of failed pregnancies. The days stretched out before me, absent of hope.

Becca was the one who told me when David started dating. Our friendship had stalled a bit from the early happy hour years, but she was always kind to me.

She'd asked if we could talk in my office. When she closed the door behind her, I knew it was bad.

"I don't know if it's serious, but I don't want you hearing it from someone else, or, God forbid, bumping into them somewhere. She's new—in the registrar's office. Young, like maybe thirty? And pretty. They look almost like brother and sister."

So she was blonde and shiny, just like David, the Barbie to his Ken. His parents would love her, those WASPs who were unfailingly polite but never warm.

Within a couple of weeks, David was blowing up my phone, asking to meet for coffee. I knew he wanted to tell me, wanted to spare my feelings. When I declined time after time, he finally texted it to me: *We're pretty serious. I don't want to hurt you. I care about you.*

My fake smile may have bled into my text: *I'm happy for you, David.*

Could I *really* be happy for him for moving on? What *choice* had I given him? I bore him no ill will.

He also reached out when they got engaged. And then married. And then pregnant. I knew he was trying to be a good guy, like his etiquette manual told him how to treat an over-the-hill ex-wife when his newer model was ready to pop out an heir.

Ever since I'd taken my position and climbed at least part way up the career ladder, to tenure and promotion to associate professor if not full, I imagined retiring from Sainsbury. I'd been there for twelve years—it was like a home to me.

As the less exciting half of a broken couple, when the more revered and famous one had moved on, I became, if not a social pariah, someone to be pitied. I always *hated* pity. A strong woman, I never asked for that "poor Marissa" bullshit.

It was my old professor who reached out to me about the job. Dr. Candace Cabrera taught Brit Lit 2 my junior year of undergrad. Though now the head of the department, she had been a new hire back then, so she hadn't been around to know about any of the drama of my first couple years of college.

Candace encouraged me to apply for grad school and even wrote me a killer recommendation. It's not like we were *close* friends, but we'd bumped into each other at some conferences over the years, and we had even collaborated on a panel presentation once. Our relationship was mostly over text, maybe a few per year, but I'd cued her in on some of my painful updates to keep her in the loop.

When Candace rang me out of the blue, even though I was pretty big on the "why call if you can text" principle, I picked up.

She didn't even say hello. "This seems like a longshot, but there's an opening for a one-year teaching position at Blackthorn."

"Hi, Candace." It was all I managed.

"I know what you're going to say. Why would you leave a tenured job to be a visiting professor with a one-year contract? I hear you."

"I didn't say anything yet." Still, my mind was already spinning.

"You seem so glum, and I know you haven't published lately. No offense. It's been a while for me, too. However, you didn't even put in for the last East Coast English Association Conference. I know because I'm on the committee, and I looked for your submission, which wasn't there."

The thing about Candace was that she still pushed me to reach my potential even though it had been ages since she was my professor. It was sweet and infuriating at the same time; she held higher standards for me than I maintained for myself.

"I've sort of been going through some stuff. And I *have* been working hard. My teaching evaluations last semester were much better."

If there was an edge to my voice, Candace ignored it. "Look, Marissa. I've known you for over twenty years now. You're stagnant. Sainsbury is no longer the right fit for you. You should consider this."

"*Candace.* Are you serious? You said it yourself. Wouldn't I be crazy to leave my career with no hope of anything permanent?"

"Wouldn't you be crazy to *stay*?"
She had me there.

---

HAVING LIVED in a pre-furnished apartment after the breakup, all it took was a U-Haul trailer hitched to my SUV and I was out of Dodge, so to speak, good old Norman in his cat carrier beside me.

After years of dealing with traffic jams and road closures in the Baltimore area, some of my heaviness lifted as I drove along the tree-lined country roads. I rolled down my windows and inhaled clean Pennsylvania air. It was a fresh start even if on familiar stomping grounds.

# Chapter 2

I hadn't stepped foot on Blackthorn University's campus since graduation over twenty years earlier. Much had changed over the years; some state-of-the-art buildings had been erected, and the ones that were bright and new back when I'd been a student had lost some of their sheen, becoming shabbier and grayer. I could relate.

Despite that, it looked regal and was as comfortable as an old pair of sweatpants compared to the stiff and formal pantsuits and business dresses I used to wear at Sainsbury.

As I gazed out across the greenery of the quad, feeling the sun on my skin and listening to the muted sounds of students talking and birds chirping, I knew my decision was the right one. I felt lighter, fuller of hope for the future than I had in years.

My nerves had been a bit jangled in the past few weeks with the stresses of settling into a new apartment, meeting colleagues, and planning curriculum, but the change tasted delicious.

No one looked at me with sad eyes or stopped whispering when I came into a room. I knew Candace wouldn't have spread my business around, and the sensation of being nearly anonymous was thrilling. Some of the faculty completely ignored me, while others were well-mannered if not friendly. Not a soul bothered me, except for Candace, and I was accustomed to her.

Candace had warned me about the apathy my colleagues would probably display upon my arrival. "Don't take it personally if the faculty aren't chomping at the bit to get to know you. They're caught up in their own work."

None of that surprised me. I had seen plenty of temporary faculty come and go over the years; with Sainsbury's reputation promising an impressive bump on their CV, people would move across the country just for a one-semester gig.

One guy I met worked in Louisiana for a semester before Sainsbury and took a job in Oregon the following year. Most of his belongings were still in storage in the south—he said he was keeping them there until he could find something permanent and would travel light in the meantime.

It wasn't a bad situation for someone unattached, and there were also perks for those who were running from something. A woman I knew moved with her teenage daughter from California for a one-semester teaching position. She told me she'd go anywhere as long as it was far away from her ex.

I told Candace as much as we drank espressos from her fancy machine. I was no longer that wilting wallflower desperate for approval, and Candace had come far from the somewhat shy adjunct professor I had met back when I was a student. We were different, more fully evolved versions of who we were back then.

Sitting in the lush armchairs across from her mahogany desk underneath the hanging decorative masks she'd picked up from her travels around the world, smelling the fresh scents of lavender from her indoor herb garden, I felt relaxed in and impressed by the elegance of Candace's office, a testament to her hard work and exotic taste.

"I won't be the least bit offended," I promised. "Trust me, I just want to support students and complete some scholarship."

Other than the few with whom I'd bonded, I hadn't gotten to know many of the temps traipsing through Sainsbury's English Department. The vast majority weren't there for long, and I didn't learn their stories. Who knew what skeletons were in their closets? And now I was one of them, a transient, an interloper, no partner or position to hold me to the area. My only plus was that, as a visiting professor with a contract, at least I had the certainty of a full academic year of employment as opposed to not knowing if there would be classes for me in the spring.

I tried to steer clear of my drama during the interview with the search committee, who'd had a difficult time understanding why I left my tenured position at Sainsbury. I didn't want it to seem like there had been a scandal, so I explained that I had lost a baby and gotten divorced. They didn't need to know the details, just my necessity for a fresh start.

I had worked so hard to secure my future at a prestigious university. Yet, my new life without the pressures of a tenure-track role, despite any promise of longevity, was exactly what I needed.

I let the benefits wash over me, happy drops of glee: optional department meetings and committee work, zero advising duties, no Saturdays spent at open house events. As long as I showed up for my classes and turned in my grades on time, I pretty much could do what I wanted. What freedom!

There was a chance I could stay on and teach more classes after my contract expired, but I could start fresh again elsewhere if the fit wasn't right. After twelve years locked in a job, flirting with options felt a lot like dating after an unhappy marriage. Not that I was ready for *that* yet, but I could picture it once I got myself together a bit more. One thing at a time.

Even better, despite my lowered salary and reduced status from tenured faculty to visiting professor, I had more control of the curriculum than ever before.

"How do you feel about teaching a class on Poe?" Candace had asked after I was officially hired. "I've been rereading some of your publications and enjoying them. I'd love for Blackthorn's students to benefit from your experience with Poe's work and your theories on his life."

"Yes!" With Blackthorn only an hour and a half from Philadelphia, I mentally started planning a field trip to the Poe house, maybe with a picnic lunch by the Wissahickon River of which Poe wrote, but the doubts soon started flooding in. "Wait, though. Aren't students already scheduled for the fall? Will anyone have space in their schedules for that class? And is there an existing class, or do I need to create one and have it get approved through the curriculum committee? Is there *time*?"

Candace laughed. "Marissa, as you *know*, Blackthorn is a small liberal arts college. It's not like Sainsbury University. We're 'way out in the willywacks,' as my mother often said, compared to Baltimore. We have an English 145 course we call 'Special Topics.' I've used that classification for some of my folklore courses over the years. The Dean of Liberal Arts was an English professor before she took her loftier position, and she's been understanding and flexible in allowing us to use this course for our passion projects.

"Come up with a title and a course description, and I'll send it out to our majors as well as to the registrar for incoming freshmen who still need electives. Trust me, your seats will be filled. I can only give you one section for now, but we'll see how it goes, and maybe we can run it again, or try something new, in the spring."

Though I had taught numerous American lit classes over

the years, I'd never been able to focus an entire course on Poe; I could only devote a single week to my specialty. Candace and I agreed that I'd teach the Poe class along with three freshman comp classes, a 4-4 load.

After brainstorming several possibilities, I came up with a course description and outline for what I called "Poe in Pennsylvania." Now that I was back in this state, I thought it would be fun to concentrate on the period when he lived in Philadelphia, some of his most productive years as a writer, and it would tie in well when we went on our trip if I could get that approved. I'd also include Poe's influence on a few Pennsylvanian writers as a way to showcase his relevance even in the twenty-first century.

As I pored over my files and books, racking my brain and scribbling different ideas in a notebook, I felt that old spark again. Even though I had thrust myself into teaching after my divorce, I had requested the same courses for the preceding three years. I'd hardly changed a thing, which had bitten me in the butt when students shared midterm exams from previous semesters with current students, creating a cheating scandal and disciplinary nightmare. Although I had been trying harder, I'd been coasting in the lesson planning department. When was the last time I'd *stretched* myself? It didn't matter—I was back.

The first day of the semester drew closer, and I slogged on, piecing together fragments of successful lesson plans and materials from over the years, revamping and streamlining and expanding as needed, patchworking a solid curriculum for each course.

I woke up early every day, utilizing the brain with which I was blessed, and made slow, steady progress figuring out how to help my students reach the learning objectives while staying engaged.

I started going for walks at dusk to watch the sunsets,

those late summer delights where the Creamsicle colors of the sky bleed in and around that burning fuchsia sun.

I even dusted off my running shoes—objects that hadn't seen the light of day in years—for an early morning couple of miles a few times a week. Though nowhere near the length of the half-marathons I used to run with David at the beginning of our marriage, these workouts were enough to feel the blood pumping through my veins, enough for me to realize that my broken heart kept on beating despite all I had lost.

I was ready, at least in part, for the next stage of my life, anxious to push past the darkness and forge ahead.

# Chapter 3

The semester got off without a hitch, more or less.

One student spun a long and fake-sounding yarn of an excuse for missing class by the second day, and another told me he could only attend remotely even though it was an in-person class, but I handled these issues, I thought, with aplomb, acknowledging the frustration of their situations but taking them back to the language in the syllabus.

These were two of my one hundred students, and most of the rest of them *seemed* reasonable. I knew from experience that a number of them would have issues at some point in the semester: deaths in the family, relationship troubles, and mental health concerns that might derail their focus from their studies, and others would lose the confidence or drive to keep going no matter how many times I reached out via email to come see me during office hours to help them get back on track. It was a professional hazard.

At least no one was telling me how much their parents had donated to the school in an inappropriate and entitled effort to gain some leverage. Students at Blackthorn were similar to those at Sainsbury in that they skipped class and made excuses for not doing their work, but they differed in socioeconomic status.

Due to the draw of in-state tuition for Pennsylvania residents, I didn't have as many cross-country or international transplants, and many more at Blackthorn were first-generation and/or underprepared. Instead of trust funds, most of Blackthorn's students were getting financial aid and figuring out student loans while working on campus or at low-paying jobs for the privilege of receiving an education.

In other words, they were different on paper from most of my former students at Sainsbury, but they weren't that different than *I* was when I came to Blackthorn, a lifetime ago, filled with the same self-doubts and financial insecurity.

By the end of the second week of the semester, I'd memorized my students' names and begun developing a rapport, getting to know them. With three freshmen comp classes, I was dealing with students experiencing the post-high school euphoria that comes with emancipation from parental guidance—and everything that entailed, from sleeping through alarms to the hangovers before Friday morning classes.

I'd seen it all before, and all I could do was encourage them to come to class.

Within the next several weeks, as we approached midterms, I found my groove with Blackthorn's students. I talked to them a little more intimately than I had at Sainsbury, understanding them differently.

"Make good choices this weekend! Remember, the best thing you can do for your grade is to come to class so you always know what's going on! I want you to be successful! And please come to office hours or email me if you're stuck!" I reminded the students in my Poe class as they hightailed it out of the room.

"You're such a mom," one of my students, a sophomore

English major named Hadley, said as she gathered up her belongings, lingering behind after the others left.

I wasn't sure how to take her comment.

"Is that bad? Or weird?" This might have felt like a gut punch even a few months before, since I was *not* actually the mother of a living child, but it didn't hit me the same way now. I hadn't alluded to my personal life in class except to say that I had a cat—there was no way Hadley would have guessed my heartbreak, and I wasn't going to let an innocuous statement propel me into an emotional tailspin. All that was behind me now. Hadley was most likely being kind.

"No! Neither! Sorry, I'm not trying to make you uncomfortable." Her eyes enlarged for a second, but then her face broke into a wide smile. "You're looking out for us but also projecting a bit of guilt so we don't disappoint you, but for our own good, like our moms do. We don't want to let you down since you care about us and just want the best for us."

She paused again, and her next words were slow, tentative, testing the waters. "You're different than a lot of the professors here. Some are just like, 'Open up your books to page thirty-four' and don't interact with us much or seem to care what we do as long as we turn in our work. Some don't even care if class is boring—they lecture at us the whole time and write a bunch of notes on the chalkboard like it's the fifties or something."

I never quite knew how to react when people complimented my teaching style, so I deflected. "I think I might have had some of those professors," I told her. "I was an English major here, too, way back when."

I didn't place myself in the same category as Dr. Fulton, an old grouch of an English professor back when I was his student. He was even older and grouchier in the present day. Still, I knew that, from a student's standpoint, anyone over about thirty-five was considered ancient, and I was as old as some of their mothers.

"Sorry if I'm talking your ear off. I know I don't talk that much in class. I get worried about what people will think if I say something that sounds dumb."

Self-doubt was common for my freshmen, but not as much for more seasoned students. I wanted to encourage her without pushing too hard. "I'd love for you to participate during discussion more. Based on your writing so far, you have a lot of thought-provoking ideas to share. In fact, I'd like you to give yourself a personal challenge of raising your hand in large group discussion next class."

Though Hadley didn't volunteer much in class, she'd worked well in groups and seemed to be right there with me every day, making strong eye contact and nodding her head when I presented new material, not on her phone or looking zoned out. These bad habits were all too common, at Sainsbury as well as at Blackthorn.

Even though my Poe class was higher interest and thus better attended than my freshmen comp classes since students had chosen it as an elective rather than forced to fill a requirement, part of me still felt disappointed when the lesson I'd tried so hard to make engaging elicited yawns rather than enthusiasm.

Hadley was quiet in class, yet she often chatted with me one-on-one afterward.

Personable but shy—I could relate. It was why I offered students opportunities to participate without having to feel like they were on center stage; my goal was never to embarrass students for what they didn't know but to build on and celebrate what they had to offer. I tried to encourage participation and make the classroom risk-tolerant so students felt comfortable and safe.

In my few short weeks at Blackthorn, I saw how important this was for my underprepared students, especially, since many lacked confidence in their abilities and weren't sure they belonged on a college campus.

"I'll *try*. I'm excited about 'The Black Cat.' I read it in middle school, and I think I'll appreciate it more now that I'm an older, more experienced reader, so maybe I'll come up with a few points to say in class next time."

"It's one of my favorites, and one of his most prominent," I said. "On our field trip to the Poe House, we'll go into the cellar that most likely inspired part of the story."

I was eager for what I had planned for the next class—a warm-up activity that was like a non-dirty, literature-based version of Cards Against Humanity to get students talking about the story. I'd used it in other lit classes I taught years ago, and it was always a hit. I was hopeful it might be fun enough to jumpstart some of my less-engaged students' interest in the class while also pushing their critical thinking skills.

"Thanks, Professor Owens. I'm glad I'm in your class this semester," Hadley said, making my heart soar a little. I was always willing to work with the students who were reluctant learners, ready to attempt to push them to reach their potential, but it was a joy when students were invested in the work on their own—when I didn't need to force it as much.

"I'm glad you're in my class, too." I waved goodbye and offered her a big smile.

Thank goodness I did. It was the last time I saw her.

# CHAPTER 4

By some marvelous stroke of coincidence, I taught my Poe class in the early evening twice a week in Grover Hall, the oldest building on campus. While erected decades after Poe's death, its Gothic-style cupola, vaulted lobby ceiling, and arched windows evoked the feeling of traveling back in time.

As an undergrad majoring in English literature and lapping up whatever I could find on Poe, anytime I'd been lucky enough to have a class in Grover, I'd imagined walking through those ornate, heavy wooden doors and following Montresor into the catacombs for a taste of that amontillado, never to see the light of day again. I pictured tombs and bodies dwelling inside instead of desks and chairs.

Then there were the campus rumors to add to the intrigue. According to the legend, back in the late 1800s, a young man named Lynn Hampstead had fallen from the front steps of Grover Hall, split his head open, and died. The story went that the stain of his blood remained after all these years, and there were repeated sightings of a student in old-fashioned attire roaming the halls at night. In the 1950s, a girl had a fatal

While I doubted the verisimilitude of the tales, I could vouch for a few facts. First, the concrete walkway did indeed bear a rust-colored hue, and that blood would *have* to be cursed to continue sullying it after more than two hundred years of Pennsylvania rain and blizzards—or maybe that discoloration had always been there.

Second, a newspaper reported that a girl named Sally Cummings died after an epileptic seizure at Blackthorn University. I remembered seeing the clipping, dated 1955 and photocopied from a microfilm machine, on a campus ghost tour long ago, though the obituary failed to specify where at the university she died.

Furthermore, I knew that the custodian who cleaned my office refused to work in Grover Hall, saying she felt a negative presence there—or maybe she didn't want to climb up on a ladder to clean the intricate crown molding. Truth be told, she left something to be desired when it came to taking out my trash regularly and cleaning the restrooms.

Exaggerated or not, these stories were the macabre icing on Miss Havisham's cobweb-covered wedding cake. Grover Hall was *perfect* for my Poe class and would gain even greater allure once darkness fell by early evening and there was more of a chill in the air. It granted me an extra spark in my quest to light a fire and leave students with a sense of elation, both for Poe's writing and the general love of learning. I couldn't wait for things to get spooky and for the giant clockface on the side of the building, observable from just about anywhere in the town of Blackthorn, to be lit up at night, its orangish glow mirroring that of a Blood Moon.

Most of the buildings at Blackthorn were pretty run-of-the-mill rectangular structures built in the 1970s, but Grover Hall's edifice graced most of the campus's marketing materials. Blackthorn students' tuition dollars kept it in excellent shape, with clean bricks, freshened mortar, and gleaming stained-glass windows.

*Inside* of Grover was another story—the old radiators couldn't quite generate enough heat in the winter with those high ceilings and drafty windows, and I doubt anyone in my sophomore year American Lit 1 class would ever forget the night a bat flew through our classroom. I'd told that story more times than I could count.

If my Poe class was lucky, history would repeat itself, and we'd have a nighttime visitor this semester. Hearing screams of terror could enhance the enjoyment of Poe's work. Based on the dramatic reactions I'd observed from students to something as unthreatening as a stink bug, a bat would cause quite a stir.

I wasn't a fan of the creatures' fingerlike paws and high-pitched chirping, but I wouldn't mind if students gained their own creepy tales to tell their friends and family while in a class devoted to the father of Gothic literature. That was the sort of thing that might make my Poe class earn a permanent spot in the course catalog.

Grover Hall was in high demand during the day by professors in various departments who wanted to teach in BU's most recognizable and prestigious building. Only the most senior faculty had that kind of pull, but they also taught during coveted hours: after ten a.m. and before dark, so they could leave early and run home to their families (or to motels to meet much younger mistresses if certain rumors were to be believed).

Without a tenure-track role, I had no control over my schedule, but I only had Norman waiting at home for me, so I didn't mind what time of day I taught. And nighttime, when darkness enveloped the campus, was far more appropriate for Poe than nine a.m.

With a spring in my step, I headed to class, raring to go,

thinking about how my students were going to love what I had in store for them that day as long as they had done their reading. Even if they hadn't, they'd probably end up enjoying their group work with the game I'd planned, and that might make them more likely to see what all the fuss was about for the next assignment.

---

I HAD SCHEDULED brief office hours directly after the night class, knowing that students often had questions right away and were more likely to show up then, rather than later. Back in the beginning of the semester, when Hadley followed me from Grover to my office in the much newer—but bland and commonplace—building of Willis Center, we talked the whole way.

"It's so exciting to have another female role model in the English Department. It makes me feel like maybe I could be a professor one day, too, if I can ever get past my stage fright. I feel comfortable with my voice when I'm writing an essay or something, but I freak out sometimes when talking in front of people. I even take pills for anxiety to help, but I'm kind of an introvert."

We were walking with a purpose, and I figured we'd get to whatever she wanted to discuss about class once we reached my office. In the meantime, we were just two people walking and making conversation, even if her compliments were over the top and making me feel a bit embarrassed.

"Hadley, I'm an introvert, too. I don't always know how to act with people in social situations. I just know that I love Poe and I love writing, so that gives me a platform. But you should see me when people make small talk. I'm hopeless."

I thought back to my own days at Blackthorn, those first few months when it seemed like everyone except me had found their true friends. At least twice a day, I'd walk into the bustling cafeteria and see tables full of laughing and grinning faces, those students lucky and popular enough to be living their best college lives. I could have tried sitting with the girl I recognized from my chemistry class, who was nice and had loaned me a pen once when mine ran out of ink, but what if she didn't want me there? I didn't want to intrude. Instead, I would stick my nose in a textbook to give the impression that I was too busy to socialize while I scarfed down cold, gelatinous pizza and watered-down Diet Coke, itching to get out of the place that reminded me of my status as an outsider.

Hadley's voice brought me back to the present, back to her.

"No, but you're cool at least. Elegant. You fit in with people."

She looked at me then, I saw, with awe and thirst for any wisdom I had to offer. She recognized me as one of her tribe, a fellow introvert, but noticed that I could coexist in the world of *belonging*.

I sighed, not wanting to get too personal or cross lines, but sometimes students reached out for validation, and I was someone who could give it to them. "What you see is only part of who I am. I used to look differently, talk differently, everything. But the most important part of me is inside all this." I waved my hand over my body; I'd let my hair go natural again, not caring enough to keep up with the straightening treatments and dye. Grays were beginning to thread through my brown strands, and I let them—it didn't feel like *me* to do something drastic, and I didn't have David in my life anymore with his subtle suggestions to maintain a certain appearance. I had the *right* to go gray if I wanted. Maybe I'd change my mind when the grays started taking over, but not yet. I felt like myself versus the facsimile I had become as David's wife, a woman with highlighted, perfectly glossy hair. My hair was wavy, dammit.

That's who I was—a woman with non-straight hair who occasionally needed to pop on a set of glasses. I was *over* contacts, and it seemed dumb to wear them all the time when I only required perfect vision for driving or looking at something off in the distance. Why stick my fingers into my eyeballs? When I kept my nails long, I felt like I might accidentally pull an Oedipus.

But the clothes stayed. Sort of. I had learned to dress in a way that flattered me, in part to my sorority days, when my Big Sister told me that my long, white socks were dorky. I'd never thought of socks as fashion statements before. Mostly, though, my fashion sense awakened from David's insistence to stop scrimping on price and buy the cut of clothes that presented me at my best.

Even without David, I had no reason to go back to my matronly khakis. Once I could fit into everything again, after the final pregnancy and that stressful period that followed, why allow my designer wardrobe to languish in my closet? While I no longer had occasions to bring out the tight cocktail dresses I had worn to David's various functions, my cashmere sweaters, tailored pants, pencil skirts, and jewelry were stylish but casual enough to help me blend in with people who thought all of that mattered.

Despite how I felt, I had learned to cultivate the *look* of success and belonging. If only the inside could match the outside.

It didn't matter, not really, especially in this new position where I no longer clamored for prestige. What counted was whether or not I knew my scholarship and could engage students' critical thinking skills while keeping them focused on the material.

Still, appearance made an impact. I didn't like to admit

how, at Sainsbury, my slender, younger form may have given me an advantage during the tenure and promotion process. We were evaluated on our teaching, scholarship, and service, and mine were solid. But I couldn't help but notice how a colleague in biochemistry, an older, slovenly woman with a similar number of publications, was denied promotion to associate professor whereas I earned it. I didn't know what her teaching evaluations were like, but I knew from word of mouth that students enjoyed her classes and respected her.

Connections also mattered. Would I have received the same accolades if I *hadn't* been David's wife? The thought that I gained something due to my relationship sat like an undercooked hamburger in my stomach, sickening me.

As I lost myself in recollections of my own troubles, Hadley was spilling her heart out. "It's just that—I don't know. I thought college would be different. My theatre teacher in high school said that everyone found their way in college, that they found their people. But I haven't really made many friends, actually."

We were outside my office. It was an awkward moment, Hadley sharing this personal tidbit as I fumbled for my keys in my purse. I'd been in this very situation before, although usually with freshmen rather than returning students, and I appreciated when students became vulnerable like this, when they saw me as someone who cared and might know how to help.

Obviously, I drew the line when they tried to use me as a therapist, having zero training in that field—I would connect them with more appropriate resources instead.

With something like this, though, students were often just looking for some kind of human connection, some authentication that they weren't weird and undeserving of friends. I agreed with Hadley's teacher that there were friends for everyone, but sometimes they could be hard to find.

I opened the door and took some time to settle my belongings while we kept talking. From experience, I knew that students didn't always feel comfortable with much eye contact when discussing such personal matters. One of my first tactics, even if it was pretty standard, was to let students know that they weren't alone in feeling friendless.

"You'd be surprised how many of my students over the years have told me that. They watched movies about college and expected to get randomly paired with a roommate who would become their best friend. I had trouble making friends and connections when I went to college, too."

My imagination had extended even farther—I thought I'd meet a glamorous friend who could give me a makeover so my ugly duckling self, with bad fashion sense and frizzy hair, would transform into a swan. I had pictured the suave roommate with her makeup palette and straightening iron instructing me on how to be my best self to make friends and find a cute boyfriend.

Now that I was talking about my own struggles in college finding friends, reaching across the decades that separated us, I took a moment to settle myself in my chair and make eye contact with Hadley, who had seated herself across the desk opposite from me.

"It's hard to believe that you had a tough time finding friends," she said, giving me a once-over. "You put yourself together so well and seem so sure of yourself."

Little did Hadley know of the girl who came to Blackthorn from a trailer park on scholarship, barely able to afford food, books, and clothes with the supplemental funding of a work-study job at the library. But she didn't need to know all *that*. That wasn't who I was anymore, but I wasn't the Carrie Bradshaw type, either.

"I *am* sure of myself when it comes to teaching, but that doesn't mean I'm always comfortable in social situations," I told her instead. All that was true—there were still times when I felt like a sore thumb sticking out when I walked into a room of people. "What about campus organizations? Are you involved with anything? That can be a great way to meet people."

This was my go-to: Let students know all of the social opportunities that awaited them! There was a club for just about every predilection.

"I was on the newspaper last semester, but that got in the way of my classes and my work schedule, so not anymore." She twisted the golden horseshoe pendant around her neck and looked at the ceiling. "I feel like all I even do is go to classes, go to work, and go back to my apartment to do homework and binge Netflix. It's kind of pathetic."

It sounded eerily similar to my own current life, but where Hadley felt lonely, I felt the freedom associated with my new start. I planned to begin hanging out at happy hours and maybe attending campus events when I was ready, but the occasional coffee or dinner with Candace was enough of a social life at that point in my post-divorce, unsettled life.

I chose my words with care; I liked Hadley and was reminded of myself at that age, but I didn't want to get too chummy with her and blur the lines between professor and friend. I had about two more minutes left in me before I diverted the conversation back to class-related matters. "It's not pathetic. Some of my best friends were people I met in classes for my major. I made friends joining study groups, and I don't care if that makes me sound geeky. And I'm still friends with some of them today."

Well, I *hoped* we were still friends. I'd ghosted a lot of folks after the events of the last couple of years. It had been easier not to talk about it to the well-intentioned people who wanted to show support but made me dwell on the darkness even more. Maybe I'd reach out to Elizabeth and Jackie and let them know I was getting back on my feet. I could suggest visiting a winery in the Poconos. Now that I was back in Pennsylvania, it wasn't too far of a drive, and I remembered there were some cute B & B's in the area. I had papers to grade, though, so maybe I'd wait until the weekend. But I *would* get in touch—I had to.

"Yeah, somebody in our class actually asked for my number, but then she just wanted my notes in case she missed class, so I'm not interested in becoming friends with her."

I knew *exactly* the kind of student she meant, the type who thought they could coast through the semester by turning in the major papers and showing up only for the midterm and final. Meanwhile, these students missed out on all the in-class activities which were part of the overall grade, not to mention the participation/attendance score. Everything was laid out in the syllabus if they'd bother looking at it.

"What about Eric? Or Dasia? Maybe Carly?" I rattled off the names of some of the stronger students in class, those I thought might have things in common with Hadley—not social misfits, but nice students who worked hard and showed a genuine inclination toward the material. "Maybe you could ask to partner up with them for group work, or I could even help make that happen if it's too awkward."

"Thanks, Dr. Owens." I noticed her ragged nails, bitten down to the quick. Like me, she was a fiddler, though nail biting was a habit I'd kicked long ago, early in my marriage, when David told me he preferred women with manicured nails. "I don't know. I don't want to come off as *desperate*."

"I'll do some creative grouping, and who knows what will happen from there." I raised my eyebrows, knowing from experience that sometimes that was all it took—a chance meeting that led to friends for life. It had happened to me, after all, back in Candace's class, when I was randomly assigned to that group of three with Jackie. Maybe Candace had done some creative grouping of her own. I'd have to ask her.

"I was thinking that maybe I'd pledge a sorority," Hadley said, avoiding my gaze. "What do you think about that?"

Oof. Good question. I had pledged, but my experience had been... complicated. I didn't think of myself as a sorority girl and doubted that I'd suggest that path for someone as socially self-conscious as Hadley.

Girls could be so *mean*. There were probably more rules and regulations at Blackthorn now after the many, many cases across the country that involved hazing, but it left a bitter taste in my mouth. "Hadley, I can't tell you what you should do. People have strong feelings both for and against Greek life. I know some people who swear by their sorority connections, but I also know some pretty terrible stories of people getting their feelings hurt when they didn't get a bid."

I decided to keep it light—I knew even worse stories when they *did*.

It was time to move this along. I appreciated the chance to buoy the confidence of a fledgling student, but there came a time and place to get focused on the task at hand: the course-work. "Let's get to business. Why don't you tell me where you're stuck on your paper?"

In retrospect, I wondered what else I could have said. Would it have mattered? Would she have listened if I told her my truths? But how *could* I have? There I was, an experienced adult, and I gave her no further advice.

Weeks later, she disappeared.

---

YEARS OF EXPERIENCE have taught me that even the best students miss class. Sometimes they reached out right away via email, and other times whatever was happening consumed them entirely, and they only emerged after it was over. I didn't think much of it when Hadley was absent the Monday after I had challenged her to participate more, though I was disappointed.

Without her, when I started class that evening, I had to move my group members around—Hadley had never taken it upon herself to reach out to the students I recommended, and I finally remembered to place her with those I thought might strike up a friendship with her. I kept looking at the door, stalling for a moment before calling out the groups for our activity, but she never came.

As I expected, my lesson went well. The students had great fun with my Cards Against Humanity-themed exercise on "The Black Cat," and I beamed seeing them leaving the room, some exchanging phone numbers and smiles with each other as they coordinated time to work on their big group project, the one that would culminate before our field trip near the end of the semester.

When Hadley missed class again on Wednesday and didn't even turn in her assignment electronically on the online learning management system, I was concerned enough to reach out. Though I didn't know her *that* well, we had connected enough that I knew she cared about her studies, and our brief interactions after class and in office hours made me feel that she might have needed someone looking out for her.

A conscientious student with a high GPA, she probably hadn't skipped class on purpose. Despite the transformation from one day to the next, from students who were uncommunicative before class, each enthralled by their phones, to the sounds of friendly chatter filling the room, Hadley's absence left a dark spot for me on this otherwise sunny horizon. When I got back to my office, I sent her a quick email.

Hi Hadley,

Just checking in. I noticed you haven't been in class this week, and you didn't turn in your paper today, so I'm concerned. I hope you are well and that I'll hear from you soon. In the meantime, please check the syllabus to keep on top of the new assignments, and let me know if you have any questions!

- Dr. Owens

I didn't reach out to *every* student when they were absent, or I'd be emailing all day, but I tried to contact them when they started missing without explanation. I knew from experience how a one-time absence could quickly escalate into a bad habit. Skipping class became easier after that first time, and then the norm became skipping versus attending, a surefire way to fail.

Sometimes, when I reached out, I could coerce a student to come back. There were those who sent me long, rambling emails at three a.m., professing their intentions to get back on track and promising to attend both class and office hours, but then... nothing. Once they started spiraling downward, few would pull themselves out of it, not even when I lent a hand to help.

I'd been wrong plenty of times before, but Hadley Parker didn't seem like the type to place anything in the way of her academic success.

As it turned out, Hadley had a great excuse, if a terrible one, for not coming to class. She couldn't. She couldn't go anywhere anymore, not to class, not to graduation, not off to grad school to pursue the idea she'd been kicking around of becoming an English professor like me.

Her mortal remains, as Poe might have put it, had taken up residence in the county morgue.

## Chapter 5

I saw it on Facebook first. Lying in bed with Norman purring away beside me a few days after my email to Hadley had gone unanswered, I was casually scrolling through social media when a post hit me like a slap in the face.

> *Have you seen her? Hadley Parker, 19 years old, is MISSING! Last seen Sunday afternoon wearing a green hoodie and jeans. Approx. 5'5" and 145 pounds. Please contact local authorities with any information.*

Some Blackthorn community group I had joined posted the message, but I learned that Hadley's roommate was the one who called the cops... eventually. I couldn't blame her—I knew a story of a girl who had been reported missing by well-intentioned friends only to turn up unharmed after a few nights of debauchery with a guy who was not her boyfriend. The girl's parents had been notified, and it became an embarrassingly miserable situation, ending with her boyfriend dumping her and her employer forcing her to get drug tested

Hadley's photograph was posted, one of those ridiculous snaps that young women made in modern days—not the Hadley I knew but a smarmy girl with her head thrown back in supposed glee as if someone had told her the world's funniest joke. A flattering, glamorous picture where her auburn hair shone and her blue eyes sparkled, it didn't capture the angst I knew she carried. This was fake Hadley. I could identify her just like I could recognize a phony version of myself in pictures, the one with the tilted head for the most flattering angle and the smile that didn't reach my eyes or show the pain I felt.

I did a Facebook deep dive, looking up information about the organization that posted as well as checking out Hadley's profile. I only accepted students as Facebook friends post-graduation, and fewer young people were on the platform lately. I didn't have full access to her information but doubted there was much to be gleaned.

Another dazzling photo. I couldn't help but wonder who took it, as it wasn't a selfie. With that flirtatious gaze and low-cut top, Hadley sure didn't look like a girl who was hurting for attention. In other words, the girl in the picture didn't seem like the one I knew, the one who had bared herself to me in her quest for companionship.

When my Poe class started on Monday, I wasn't the only one looking at Hadley's empty seat. Someone can go missing and turn up unharmed. But, by this stage of my life, much of my optimism had perished, and part of me was always attuned to expect the worst, to wait for that other shoe to drop.

And it did, that very night.

Sitting in front of my computer grading papers, I heard my phone buzz with an incoming text from Candace: *Check your email. Is this your student?*

I hadn't talked to Candace in the last week. That wasn't unusual in our busy lives, and I appreciated how Candace kept herself almost at arm's length instead of being one of those people who demands intimacy from their friends. I must have said something to her earlier about Hadley, or maybe she'd looked up her schedule. My heart seeming to pound in my ears, I opened up my email.

The president of the university, a man I hadn't met in my status as a lowly visiting professor, had sent out the following message:

Dear Campus Community,

It is with great sadness that I share the passing of one of our beloved students. Hadley Parker was a sophomore English major from York, Pennsylvania. Her body was found today in Water's Edge State Park. Police are looking into the matter.

If you have any information regarding Hadley's disappearance and subsequent death, please reach out to the Blackthorn Police Department. Also, please contact the Center for Counseling if you require support.

I hope you will join me in your thoughts and/or prayers for the healing of Hadley's friends and family.

Sincerely,

Andrew Lattimore, Ph.D.

President, Blackthorn University

I slammed my laptop shut, as if that would erase what I had just read.

That sweet girl, gone, wiped out, her future decimated, and her body lying out in the cold, most likely for several days. I wondered who had found her—a hiker, maybe, or had the police been out looking since she was reported missing? Should I have started a search party, or at least looked to see if there was one I could join? Would that even have *mattered* if she were already dead?

The president had provided scant information, so I had no idea if it had been an accident or something far worse. "Police are looking into the matter" could mean *any*thing. Police were involved in everything from minor fender benders to homicides. Was it significant that the local police versus the university police were on the case, if this even counted as a case? I didn't know, as most—not all, but most—of my police interactions involved running red lights or speeding.

I mulled over my final conversations with Hadley. She had mentioned trouble finding friends. Was she depressed and maybe suicidal? But I remembered her saying she was looking forward to the reading. Did people who were thinking about killing themselves make future plans? And why would Hadley drive all the way to Water's Edge to do it? I was speculating—there was nothing that said *how* she had died. For all I knew, she fell during a hike.

A Google search offered me no answers. The local papers and stations only mentioned her disappearance, nothing on the cause of death or facts surrounding the case. All I knew for sure was when she was reported missing and that the body was found this morning, a time she should have been making a Starbucks run and heading off to class.

I slept fitfully that night, thinking of the two Hadleys: the confident-looking one in the pictures versus the girl I knew with big dreams but even bigger insecurities. And I thought of her family, the people who would forevermore have one empty spot at their table at holiday gatherings, the family whose entire lives had changed.

Hadley was gone—nothing could change that. I just hoped her parents would receive some answers as to what had happened to wipe out that smart, shy, inquisitive girl. I wanted answers, too.

# Chapter 6

## Then

Marissa never planned on pledging a sorority.

It all sounded so stupid—buy your friends! Wear dumb jackets so everyone knows you're part of a group!

But she also didn't expect the feeling of abandonment she experienced at the end of freshman year when her various dormmates paired off as roommates with members of their sororities or sports teams.

As April rolled into May, she thought she had a concrete plan: Amber, her close friend from her dorm floor, and she were getting a place off campus with a couple of girls from Amber's volleyball team. Although Marissa couldn't spike a ball if her life depended on it, she knew the volleyball girls; she'd hung out with them all year. Their friendships were solid.

Call it her sixth sense, or maybe it was just her imposter syndrome, but part of her knew she didn't fit in, and not just because she was petite. For a bunch of volleyball girls, most members of this crew were pretty damn short, as well, except for Paige, who towered over the rest of them like a giraffe amongst cats. And Marissa always supported them, even though watching sports was never her thing—she couldn't count how many times she sat in those bleachers by herself to cheer for Amber, and, by extension, her friends and teammates.

But was Amber there for Marissa? Not when it came down to it.

Amber's face looked stricken, her mouth pinched and puckered, when she told Marissa the news. If it wasn't so incredibly hurtful, almost like a breakup, Marissa would've wanted to comfort her friend, maybe get her a coffee and a cookie or something, just so that sad look wouldn't besmirch her wide-set, innocent-looking farmgirl eyes.

She had told Marissa they needed to talk. "I'm sorry, but we can't be roommates next year. I know it was supposed to be us and Randi and Chelsea in the off-campus apartment, and I know how much time you spent looking for a place for us, but I can't. Randi and Chelsea and I were asked to move into the volleyball house." Amber looked down, away from Marissa's eyes, which were probably bugging out as she tried not to panic, to not allow the stress of the situation to show its ugly self upon her face. "You won't be able to live with us since you're not on the team."

Marissa exhaled then, just one breath, before she reined it in. She had been petrified at the beginning of the year that she wouldn't make friends, that she wouldn't fit in, but she had found her tribe, or so she thought.

Amber continued. "You know I love you, right?" She attempted to smile, but her thin lips still held that twisted quality. "I really *wanted* to room with you. But now Randi and Chelsea wanna take this opportunity, and I have to go with them. I'm so, so sorry." For emphasis, she chewed a cuticle. Her nails were a mess.

Amber was right: Marissa wasn't on the team, so she

couldn't live there. Could she blame Amber? Not in fairness, but it still hurt.

Marissa dug her fingernails into the palms of her hands, willing back the tears threatening to spill. She learned to do this long ago, back in junior high when a classmate had picked on her for being too sensitive. Despite everything, she found herself nodding, making soothing noises, and worrying about her friend's feelings, even though Amber was the one with a place to live while she languished alone.

"Yeah, too bad I never got into that volleyball thing. It's fine. I'll figure it out." She wondered if the smile plastered on her face for Amber's benefit looked as artificial as it felt.

---

MARISSA NEVER LET Amber know how alone and betrayed it made her feel. She knew Amber wasn't trying to be cruel—she just had no idea how it affected her friend. She didn't grow up like Marissa, didn't know what it was like to feel unloved or like a burden. There was no point expressing all that messiness. She preferred acting like it wasn't blowing up her entire existence.

She'd have to contact residence life and allow herself to be placed randomly with a new roommate in the dorm the next year. It would be a little embarrassing that she couldn't find her own roommate, but it wasn't like Marissa was some social climber trying to prove anything to anyone.

Part of her felt like she should have pledged earlier in the semester when she had the chance; then she wouldn't be dealing with this now. Marissa and her roommate, Scarlett, had gone through rush together early in the spring semester to check out the sororities.

Marissa found it all very unnerving: the phoniness and

small talk, the sisters in the various organizations seeming to assess every bit of each rushee and tally it up on a scorecard.

At that point in Marissa's life, she didn't have much confidence. Her name-brand clothes, items from Gap and Limited Express, mostly came from Goodwill and were likely a season or two out of style. She didn't really know how to put outfits together despite poring over *Seventeen* magazine. She had some crazy notion in her head that she could belong to one of those upper-crust organizations, that she could trick these girls into thinking she fit in. But, when it came down to it, they saw right through her.

Marissa ate the cucumber sandwiches and tried not to get crumbs in her hair. She smiled and laughed at the vacuous jokes and pretended to enjoy herself. At some level, though, she knew those sororities weren't for her.

Scarlett and Marissa went into rush pretty blind, not knowing a soul in any of the organizations and ignoring preconceived ideas. But, at the different houses, Marissa got a feel for what could have been. *What if* she were born to money? *What if* she contained that unknown quality, that "it girl" appeal that made people want to spend time with her? Those sorority girls with their perfectly shaped eyebrows, flat stomachs, and tiny crop tops seemed to know how the world worked, and Marissa wanted in.

Giddy with anticipation after a brief stop at their dorm to freshen up, Scarlett and Marissa tested the waters.

"I want Sig Omicron the most, I think," Scarlett said, "but I'll take anything. I just want to get in *some*where. Will you pledge with me, roomie? Pretty, pretty please?" She batted her eyelashes.

Marissa knew that Sig Omicron was only a fantasy for Scarlett, with her wide hips, broad nose, and flat chest. If there was one sorority on campus that prided appearance over everything, it was Sig Om.

"I don't know. I don't know what I want."

This was at least half true. Marissa knew she wanted to be accepted, but she was a little more realistic than her roommate. Conventionally, at least, she was attractive—was it enough? If not, was she willing to settle for another sorority that wasn't the top tier?

When they both received bids for Tri Pi, Scarlett was thrilled. It was the only bid Scarlett received, and she didn't care.

"I *knew* I liked them the best. They're the nicest." Scarlett hadn't even been holding her breath when Sig Om read the names of whom they were granting bids. But Marissa had, and when the tall, chic president of Sig Om didn't read her name, she felt her world cave in a little. She didn't know for sure if she'd have accepted, but the fact that they didn't want her stung.

Marissa ended up receiving three bids to Scarlett's one, but those endorsements failed to dull the pain of rejection. The rushees had two hours to decide if and where they wanted to pledge.

Marissa changed into her pajamas early despite Scarlett's pleas to pledge Tri Pi with her. She claimed she wasn't feeling well and that the pledging thing wasn't for her, anyway. She went to bed and pretended to be asleep when Scarlett came back home, green and white balloons in hand, gushing with happiness and exhilaration.

And, since she didn't pledge that semester, she threw herself into those friendships with the volleyball girls, who generally shunned the sorority types. But then they deserted her, too, even if they didn't mean to, and Marissa was all alone again.

## CHAPTER 7

I t didn't feel right going to campus the next morning. Tragedy had befallen students at Blackthorn, as well as at every other institution of higher learning, as long as the university existed—whether from car accidents, diseases, or something more nefarious, as Hadley's death may have been. Sometimes students died, but classes were never canceled. The rest of us had to keep living and breathing, performing all of our mundane tasks like brushing our teeth, filling up our cars with gas, and doing laundry while Hadley's life was extinguished, a bright flame snuffed out.

Though I shed no tears for Hadley, I carried the heaviness of her loss like a thick cloak on my shoulders, weighing me down and casting a gloomy pall over everything. My mind manufactured terrible pictures of her ruined body in the woods.

Hadley wasn't mine to mourn, not really—she had family and friends who loved her. Her absence would cause far bigger vacancies in their hearts than mine; I was only her professor, and I could count her presence in my life in mere weeks. But that wouldn't make the empty desk in my classroom any easier.

Normally, since my class started at two o'clock, I would stay at home on Tuesdays until almost noon, enjoying coffee and a little reading in bed before showering and putting on real clothes.

This particular morning, though, I didn't want to luxuriate at home, even though I had a bigger workspace than my closet-like office provided me. I was usually there for office hours and not much more, but I figured I should arrive at campus early in case there were special instructions for those of us who had Hadley in our classes. I doubted it—maybe that email from the president was all we would receive on the matter. I'd never had one of my current students pass away in all my years of teaching, so I didn't know if there were some sort of guidelines for the situation.

Over the years, after presidential announcements like the one I read last night, I'd heard some chatter about students who died. I'd also received emails from my students asking for extensions on papers since they were grieving for a lost friend. Generally, I'd grant these—I was big on documentation, but what was I supposed to do in cases like those, demand a photo of the student with the deceased to prove they were friends?

The truth was that I'd always felt a rush of relief, after my original feeling of sadness, when I read a grim email: sad for the loss of life of a young person but glad it wasn't someone I knew. It was easy enough to move on when the misfortune wasn't my own, and I'd never discussed a student's death in class. At Sainsbury, with its giant population, it was unlikely anyone in my class would have known the unfortunate student.

Now, though, my entire class knew the student who had died. Her empty seat would take up more space and attention than Hadley herself ever had, but it was a small class and they knew who she was, saw her every day since she sat right in the front. Since our talk that one time when she mentioned not having friends, I didn't believe she had become chummy with anyone from class, but it was possible. Even the casual act of saying hello or lending a piece of paper might be enough to trigger a reaction to her loss in one of her classmates.

Many of my students came from underprivileged backgrounds, and my guess was they had experienced quite a bit of turmoil even at their young ages. For some, maybe this would be one more notch in a string of tragic stories.

Another adjunct I met, a friendly, middle-aged woman who taught in the College of Education and enjoyed a Starbucks latte as much as I did, told me that her full-time job was as a high school teacher. I don't know why she brought this up in line for coffee—maybe it was her mission to try to help faculty better understand their students—but she said that her inner-city students were plagued by issues including drug and gun violence. They wrote about it in their essays, how they had lost a brother to an overdose or hadn't seen their mother in years since she was locked up. They were desperate for a way out, and she encouraged them to apply to Blackthorn, but many of her former students ended up dropping out after their freshman year, unable to juggle their professors' requests with the demands to contribute to their families and sort out problems at home.

I enjoyed bumping into her on occasion. She wasn't so serious all the time, and I respected her need to educate, to advocate for our students. But if she viewed me as a woman in an ivory tower who didn't understand the struggles of poverty, she was wrong. Dead wrong.

Then again, that's what I wanted, wasn't it? To separate myself from my past? To hide the quiet, timid girl behind a wealthier-looking veneer? I couldn't blame this woman for thinking I was one of *those* professors, one who assumed that all of their students grew up in stable homes with parents who doted on them, providing the dual commodities of money and love. No, that wasn't who I was, not at all. But how could I justify feeling sorry for myself when I was living and breathing?

After deciding on business as usual in my composition class, full of freshmen who probably didn't know Hadley, I tried to figure out a plan for my Poe class the next day. Though I'd personally lost a classmate before, I'd never been on the other side of the podium. I couldn't act as if everything was normal—that would be callous. Then again, I wasn't a counselor, and students were paying their hard-earned tuition dollars for class. The show had to go on.

The scheduled reading for discussion for the class the next day was "The Masque of the Red Death," one of my favorites. But how could we talk about foolish Prince Prospero, the gruesome stranger, and the ebony clock ticking away when one of our own class members had just died, when her time had run out? It didn't seem appropriate.

But what else would we talk about in a Poe class? When I read that story back in high school, my sweet but ditzy English teacher had given us two whole class periods to craft elaborate masks. It was fun, and mine looked pretty incredible, but there was barely any discussion of the story and zero learning. Nope, I wouldn't be doing *that*.

I was deep in thought, brainstorming ideas and crossing them out on a notepad, when there was a knock on my open office door. It was Candace, her slim body a silhouette in the doorway, her mouth a thin line under knitted brows.

"Marissa, I wanted to check in with you. The president asked all the chairs to touch base with faculty who taught the, uh, deceased student."

*Deceased student.* Even if she were trying to be more

respectful, the term felt colder and less personal than saying Hadley's name.

"Thank you," I replied. "The news is quite a shock."

She climbed into one of the chairs crammed into the small space looking pale and almost ghostly, as if she, too, were suffering from Hadley's loss. "I've worked here a long time. This particular case looks like there could be some blowback for Blackthorn. Already, according to the president, parents are swarming social media asking if their children are safe here."

"Does that mean they discovered foul play?" I felt like I was reciting a line from a TV show. How was this real life, *my* life, my student?

Candace threw her hands in the air and shook her head, her well-maintained blonde bob swinging back and forth. "If Lattimore knows anything, if the police have given him any clues, he didn't share them. It was a small meeting, just the chairs, the top administrators, and the legal people. If you ask me, the president had been primed by his team on what he should say to us, so I'm here to pass it on to you. We were to 'check in' with our faculty and see if you needed anything." She made air quotes and rolled her eyes, seeming discontent with the lack of specificity in those directions.

"Thank you," I said again. What *could* I need? Counseling? A hug? How about a cookie? I felt sad, but, again, Hadley's loss wasn't really mine. Maybe I'd picture her young, earnest face and feel guilty for not doing more, but I wasn't entitled to any special treatment.

"Back to the backlash thing. The police might come by to question you as one of Hadley's professors. I don't know how likely that is, but Lattimore wanted us to give you a warning." Candace pursed her thin lips, searching for the words. "Not a *warning*, exactly, more of a heads-up. Most of our faculty haven't interacted with the police more than to argue about a speeding ticket, and they're definitely not used to being interviewed by detectives."

Here were some assumptions again, lumping me into a group of people with far different experiences than my own. A shiver ran down my spine when I remembered the last time I'd talked to a detective.

"Hopefully it's just an accident," I murmured. Dead is dead, but some deaths are easier to swallow than others. Some deaths weigh lighter on one's conscience.

"If they talk to you, just try to say what you know about the young lady. Don't be nervous, and don't hold anything back—if she told you any details about her life, if she wrote anything of interest in her papers. They might ask you for her work, and you should give it to them. Trust me. We need to fully cooperate."

"Why would I be nervous? It's not like I had anything to do with what happened. She was my student, that's all." The words flew out of my mouth before I could stop them, my tone that of a petulant child rather than a professional. Old habits die hard—the need to be defensive even when no one was accusing me of anything. "Sorry, this business is just awful, and I guess I'm figuring out how to deal with it. And I *did* care for her. I had gotten to know her pretty well. She spent a bunch of time with me during office hours. She was a nice girl, and I'm both sad and angry that this has happened. *Especially* if there's someone else involved."

Candace's face contorted briefly in surprise at my outburst before rearranging itself into an expression of concern. She reached out her manicured fingers and placed them on top of mine just for a moment before I slid my hand away, unused to even a small touch from another human. "These things can hit hard, Marissa."

A pregnant pause hung in the air after that massive understatement. Candace's eyes darted around my tiny space, taking in the lack of adornment. No photos graced my walls—of whom would I display a picture, myself? But that wasn't so different from Candace's own lack of personal touches in her office; despite the lavish furniture and exotic knickknacks, she was also a loner without the ubiquitous family photos many of our colleagues displayed for the world to see.

I had completed the work order so that my framed degrees and portrait of Poe hung on the walls, nearly taking up the entire area. Years ago, David had commissioned the work from a resident artist, and it captured Poe perfectly even in an expressionist style, the gaunt face and haunted eyes that seemed to capture his pain.

While I had sold most of the jewelry David had gifted me when we were together, not wanting the ghosts of his love to touch my flesh so intimately, I would never let go of this dark and tortured portrait.

Candace said nothing other than, "Fascinating painting," even though she'd been in my office several times and must have seen it before. She hauled herself out of the chair, nodding as she left, as if the matter were settled.

I hoped so. I hoped the police would learn that it was a terrible accident, a slip from a lone and inexperienced hiker, only this and nothing more.

When two men in suits came tapping, tapping at my chamber door, I guessed they'd discovered it wasn't an accident after all.

# Chapter 8

It happened right after I had finished teaching my freshman comp class for the day, one where I pretended not to overhear the gossipy quips from students as they shared theories about how "that girl" died. What could I say? They didn't know her. It was a true crime podcast come to life for them, maybe. The excitement in their voices sounded so inappropriate, so revolting, but I couldn't get myself together enough to say something wise about human frailty, to quash their revelry with a resolute truth about "that girl." She had a name. Her name was Hadley, and she was more than a piece of chatter for students to toss about like a hacky sack.

So we practiced integrating partial quotes into sentences and went over in-text citation for maybe the twentieth time. Many still weren't getting it. They weren't getting a lot, the ones who skipped class often and never came to office hours, but I had to compartmentalize my feelings rather than get outed on TikTok, Yik Yak, or some other inane-sounding social media forum as the professor who lost it during class.

I knew the men blocking out the light in my doorway were detectives since they weren't in uniforms. Accustomed to

David's highfalutin' tastes, I could tell these guys' suits were more Men's Warehouse or Kohl's than Armani. Still, they carried an air of authority about them that our Blackthorn University PD, mostly in charge of parking tickets as far as I knew, did not.

"Ms. Owens?" the younger of the two asked me, flashing his badge in unison with his partner, a synchronized effort that might have been comical under other circumstances. He was probably around my age judging by the crinkles near his eyes and white-tinged sideburns. He wore his bargain suit about as well as could be expected and definitely better than his partner, a sixty-ish guy with a receding hairline and advancing gut.

They both stared at me expectantly as I gathered the papers on my desk. Even though Candace had clued me in, it was still alarming to see these two in my office.

"Dr.," I corrected. I couldn't help it. I wasn't *trying* to get off to a bad start, but I had vowed a long time ago to advocate for myself. Like many other female academics, students and even professionals were quick to regard me as "Ms., Miss, or Mrs." while calling my male colleagues Dr. or Professor even if their credentials didn't line up—not that I ever heard those men correcting a reference to an unearned title. I even had one former colleague, a trust fund type who received an honorary doctorate after a generous donation, demand to be called Dr. when he hadn't earned the degree.

"Excuse me, *Dr.* Owens." I couldn't read his tone to tell if it was annoyance, impatience, or embarrassment on his part. At least he didn't roll his eyes. "I'm Detective Ruiz, and this is my partner Detective Welch. We're here to discuss your relationship with the decedent, Hadley Parker."

"Okay. She was my student," I began, distracted. "Does the fact that you're here mean you think it wasn't an accident?"

"We are not at liberty to discuss that information at this

time," Welch replied, his baritone voice sounding bored. During his career, he may have repeated that line hundreds of times for all I knew.

"At this point, we're gathering information, trying to understand who Hadley was and what happened to her." Ruiz's voice sounded kinder than Welch's, and I wondered if they were already pulling a good cop/bad cop routine on me. But why would they? I was her professor, not a jealous boyfriend or rival or something. "We're reaching out to all of her professors. But, the truth is, you're the priority. We are *most* interested in speaking with you, Dr. Owens."

He let the words sit there for a moment before proceeding. "The university gave us access to Hadley's email account, so we're sifting through everything from the last few months. Most of what we've found is pretty standard—coupons for the bookstore, whole-class emails from various professors, copy-paste type of check-ins from her advisor. That kind of thing. But, from you, we saw some emails that seemed awfully friendly and personal."

"I like to be *personable* with my students. I don't think there's anything unusual in that." My words came out clipped, defensive, not sure where this was going. *I can't possibly be a suspect, can I? What on earth would my motive be?*

Ruiz cleared his throat and started again, softer this time. "What I *mean* is that you may have been one of the only adults who had gotten to know her as more than a body in your classroom."

He pulled out a notebook—so small that I imagined he'd need a new one after today's interviews alone—from his back pocket and flipped through the pages. Welch stood by, solemn and soundless, waiting while his partner found whatever he was searching for. "You see, Dr. Owens, our preliminary investigation, our *very* preliminary investigation, has turned up some information implying that Hadley was a bit of a loner, the kind of student who gets good grades but keeps to herself. So, let's start with that. May we sit?"

I nodded my consent, and the two men settled themselves in, the three of us crowding the small space and Welch's girth causing him to contort his body in the Goldilocks-like chair.

"Tell us what Hadley was like in class." It was a command now, the gentle tone gone.

"She was quiet, rarely speaking in class discussion, but it was because she was shy, not uncaring. She was always right there with me during a lesson." I pictured Hadley, always alert and engaged, throughout the lecture portions of class. "Her eye contact was excellent, and she was never off-task like some students are, looking up other stuff on their laptops or checking their phones. I always knew she *wanted* to participate —she had so much to offer. She was just too shy."

"And why do you keep saying 'shy'? How can you judge that?"

"She *told* me. She'd often stay and chat for a few minutes after class, telling me things she wanted to say in class but didn't get the courage to share. I think she wanted my approval and tried to show me how involved her mind was. I gave her the challenge to raise her hand during class discussion, but she asked me to please not call on her because of her anxiety. She told me she took medication for it." I flushed, wondering if I'd just committed a FERPA violation.

Apparently, Welch *was* paying attention. "Yes, you're allowed to share that with us. The toxicology report will tell us everything in a few days."

"Tell me about your office hour meetings," Ruiz pressed. "Why did Hadley come to you? Did she need a lot of extra help? Was she struggling in your class, or was it something else?"

I sighed, sensing where he was going, what he wanted from me. It felt like a betrayal, divulging what she confided to me. But what if this led them to a clue about what had happened?

"She had a lot of questions and demanded excellence from herself. It didn't matter that she had done well on every assignment—she wanted to turn in superior work, and I also think she trusted me and needed a human connection. In fact, a few weeks ago she sat right there, where you're sitting, Detective Welch, and told me she was having trouble making friends." How I wished Hadley was there instead of these two intrusive men.

Ruiz didn't change his expression, didn't sit up on the edge of the seat, but his left eyelid twitched in response. "That seems like quite the confession. Do many students tell their professors such intimate details about their lives, or would you say that the two of you had a relationship more as friends than teacher and student?"

My annoyance bubbled to the surface. "No, Detective Ruiz, we weren't *friends*. We had an appropriate and professional relationship, yet you might be surprised at how often office hours veer from talking about an upcoming essay to other problems the students are experiencing. I've had many students in my office over the years telling me about their social problems. I try to indulge them a bit and offer some support, suggest some resources at the university, but I don't host therapy sessions or have 'girl talk' in my professional office. I don't know if you're insinuating that my relationship with Hadley was anything but appropriate." There, I said it.

Ruiz performed that awful hand motion men use that implies *calm down*. "Nothing of the sort. We're all on the same side here, trying to find out what happened to this promising young woman. Do you remember if you gave her any advice on how to make friends?"

I wanted off this merry-go-round of Ruiz playing both

roles, good cop and bad cop, while Welch, stoic, may have been nodding off.

"Yes, I remember, because, as I said, this is a common problem. I tell students they should think about forming study groups with members of their class to make some connections, and I ask them general questions like, 'Are you involved in any clubs or activities?' and they usually say no. So, I start listing some clubs to join to be more active—the literary magazine or newspaper if they enjoy writing, intramural sports if they're athletic, organizations associated with their major, things like that. They often don't know these opportunities exist, so I try to let them know so they can meet others who share their interests."

I felt my cheeks grow hot again and wondered if I was focusing too much on myself versus Hadley. They didn't care if I was a good mentor or not; it wasn't relevant.

"Good, good." Ruiz scribbled something in that Barbie-sized notebook. "Do you recall if Hadley acted interested in any of your suggestions?"

"I also told her I'd put her in a group with some other students I thought might be good friend matches for her, but she seemed a little awkward about that, like it might be obvious I was playing matchmaker. And then I never actually did it. Well, I had planned to group her with certain students last Monday, but that was when she missed class for the first time."

The knowledge that she was probably already dead by then transmitted shards of ice into my veins. "And then she told me she was thinking about pledging a sorority. She wanted to know what I thought about that."

Another hand movement from Ruiz, this time to keep going. "And? What did you tell her? Did you encourage it one way or the other?"

"No, Detective. I don't mother my students," I said

despite remembering Hadley saying I was like a mom. "I won't tell them what they should and shouldn't do. I told her she needed to make her own choices, that I knew people with both good and bad things to say about Greek life." *Watch a Lifetime movie*, I wanted to tell him.

"How long ago, approximately, did you and Hadley have this conversation? Could you narrow it down to the week, maybe?"

"It had to have been a Monday—that's the day I have office hours right after her class. And it wasn't the first week, but it was early on, so maybe the second?" I checked my calendar on my phone. "August 29, I think."

"And she missed your class on October 3, eight days ago. So five weeks in between her telling you this and disappearing."

He motioned to his partner that it was time to leave, got up, straightened his turquoise tie, and put away his notebook. He reached out his hand to shake mine, which he hadn't done upon first meeting me. This made it twice that my hand was touched in one day. His was warm but dry, unlike Candace's rather clammy paw.

"Thank you, Dr. Owens. This has been extremely helpful. We'll be in touch, and don't hesitate to give me a call if you think of anything else." He placed a business card on my desk and exited, Welch trailing behind him, a St. Bernard at his master's heels.

*Detective Jake Ruiz, Blackthorn Police Department, Homicide* the card read.

Homicide. So they *had* found something.

# CHAPTER 9

*F*ocus. *Block it out.* I needed a minute to close my office door for privacy—not that any of my students were coming for office hours that day, anyway, and not that the police cared they were infringing upon my contractual time devoted to students. I was glad no one came that day. What would I have told them? *Sorry, can't talk about your little essay right now. I need to help these detectives solve a murder.*

I lay my head on the desk, wanting to feel the cool, fake wood for a minute or two to ground myself, and then I packed my belongings and left.

*Weird* is the only word to describe how I felt on my short drive back to my apartment. I wasn't happy with how the interview went—I couldn't get a handle on Ruiz and where he was going. He pissed me off with that singular routine, the way he seemed to insinuate an unseemly relationship. My skin crawled at the notion that I was anything other than who I claimed to be: a professor who cared about her students and wanted them to feel a sense of belonging at the university. Was that so wrong?

When I reached home, I poured myself a glass of pino

grigio, an atypical beverage for a Tuesday night. With my genetic history, alcohol was best consumed, if at all, irregularly.

As I watched the pale, yellow liquid fill the glass, I couldn't help but think about my childhood. I could see myself back in that cramped kitchen with the heaps of dirty dishes in the sink and covering the counter, last night's Kraft Mac & Cheese congealing into rock-hard mounds in the pot. If I offered to help, Mom would say I was doing it wrong; she preferred to clean up on her own time—when there weren't any dishes left—and curse at the rest of us for our laziness.

"Rissa, bring me another Jack and Coke." Dad knew I hated the nickname, but it was better than Miss Priss, which he and Mom both called me when they thought I was "acting grown."

After dumping the dregs of his drink, I dragged the chair over to the fridge and stood on tiptoes to reach the cabinet above. Two ice cubes, heavy on the Jack, light on the Coke. I was the best eight-year-old bartender I knew.

"And here you are, sir." I placed a cocktail napkin under the glass. He liked that—it was part of the game, like he was out at a real bar instead of stuck in this trailer with his wife and daughters.

"Thank you." He smiled, and I glimpsed the man he used to be, the fun dad I remembered from before the car accident that messed up his back and gave him constant pain. But I saw the glaze settling over his eyes and knew it wouldn't be long before he and Mom started nitpicking at each other: his drinking, her nagging. The booze loosened his tongue and piqued her anger. They both blamed the other for their unhappiness.

I glanced at Annie, content in her six-year-old oblivion, curled up on the couch, eyes glued to the TV as Matlock unearthed the true killer. I'd tuck her into bed soon and play her favorite cassette so she wouldn't hear the yelling.

Bringing myself back to the present, I focused on a new mantra: *You are not your parents. And you are not your past.*

I fed Norman his kibble and drank my wine, careful to take measured sips, stopping after two glasses when it was just enough to let me feel some separation from myself, from all these emotions rushing at me.

---

I WAS RESTLESS ALL NIGHT, having violent dreams during the moments I managed to sleep. Though I couldn't remember what they were, I woke up in a cold sweat with my heart racing, thinking about the warm, sticky sensation of blood on my hands.

At five a.m., I gave up trying to sleep and arose, making myself a cup of coffee. My brain throbbed with exhaustion, those two glasses of wine, and thoughts related to Hadley's death, so it was sheer willpower alone that dragged me to my desk to figure out my lesson plan.

In general, I followed a rule to plan my lessons and make photocopies for the next week before going home on a Friday, and I *had* been prepared, but I wanted to handle my Poe class differently in light of what had happened. No further communication had transpired from the university regarding how I should address Hadley's death in class.

Perhaps I should have counted my lucky stars that I'd get to control how to handle it, rather than having a counselor, administrator, or even the detectives, none of whom had even known Hadley, come in to offer false platitudes about the person she was.

It was all up to me. *I* controlled the narrative. But what would I say?

By seven a.m., I had no additional answers, just a bunch more scribbled-out ideas on my notepad, but the sun was finally rising. I quickly dressed for a short run, forgoing my headphones. At times, I needed the sound of my thoughts in my head, without the distraction of music, to figure something out.

I wasn't always a good communicator. I could talk about Poe or MLA citations until I was blue in the face, but I struggled expressing my emotions. Even when experiencing genuine sentiments, I had spent so long repressing feelings that I knew I could appear austere and uncaring. That's what I'd been told, anyway, and not only by my ex-husband. I had to get it right in class that day.

My breath caught a bit in my chest, reminding me that I possessed lungs with a light touch of asthma. But, as I inhaled the fresh, crisp Pennsylvania air and gazed up at the trees metamorphosing into kaleidoscopic hues, and as my muscles strained and stretched, pushing myself to tread farther and faster, I felt alive and ready to face the challenge of ushering my students through this terrible time.

FORTIFIED WITH ENDORPHINS, not to mention the success of two particularly engaged freshman comp classes that morning, I was as ready as could be expected when students trickled into my Poe class early that evening. I never assigned seats, but most students were territorial and sat in the same exact place every time. On this day, though, the emptiness in Hadley's former seat extended out, tentaclelike, and no one sat at the desks surrounding hers, as if the misfortune that befell Hadley were contagious.

No one approached me before class to ask a question or offer some chit chat, per the norm, and nor did the class buzz with the singsong gossipy cheer of my other classes. For this, I was glad. Even if these students hadn't known Hadley well, they had sat with her in class every day and factored into her short life.

At exactly five o'clock, as always, I began, though my voice sounded reedy and timorous. "I want to acknowledge the loss of our classmate, Hadley Parker. I'm sure you've all heard by now that she died. It's horrible and shocking, and we don't know the details. I hope that some of you got to know Hadley or at least interact with her in some way. I can tell you that she was an excellent student and a kind person. I've been teaching for a long time and have never lost a current student, so I'm feeling upset and confused about what happened. Please don't feel obligated or put on the spot, but does anyone want to say anything about Hadley?"

The students shuffled in their seats, some looking down at their desks and others staring at spots on the wall behind me. Based on our conversation, I knew Hadley felt timid in this class, but she had at least talked to some other students during collaborative group work, and it seemed appropriate to give her classmates the opportunity to speak. The articles I had read on the subject suggested that I should say something regarding my own attempts to process what happened and also offer students a chance to talk about it if they wanted to. I waited as the hot tension of uncomfortable silence suffused the air.

Finally, a girl raised her hand. "I didn't really know Hadley, but I worked with her a few times in class when you had us do partner work, since we sit near each other. *Sat.*" Brielle was one of the students who had relocated to another, farther away seat from Hadley's empty desk. "She had so much to say about Poe's stories that it actually made me go back and read them more closely. She seemed so excited, just by the words, and it made me think I must have missed something. She was the kind of student I'd like to be. I want to care that much about school, and, like, literature and stuff. I bet I'll think about her forever when I read Poe's works."

She smiled, a downcast one. "I'll think of her forevermore."

"Thank you, Brielle, that was touching," I said, raising my eyebrows in an "Anyone else?" gesture.

Jamar raised his hand next. "I never worked with her in this class, but I sat next to her in sociology last year, and she was nice. Like, she'd give you a tissue or cough drop if she saw someone needed it, or a pen or something. She was a person who just seemed *good*, but I never even talked to her other than 'hi,' and now she's gone forever, and no one even knows what happened. Did someone do this to her, Professor? Did someone *kill* that nice girl?"

"I don't know, Jamar." My mind flashed back to that word on Ruiz's business card: *homicide*. The detectives hadn't said to keep it a secret that they had talked to me, but I didn't want to fuel any rumors. "The police are looking into it and asking questions. Hopefully, they'll get to the bottom of whatever happened, and then we'll all get some answers."

It went on like that for a few minutes, students sharing memories of how Hadley was so "nice" and "smart." I respected the reverent way in which they handled the talk; unlike my one freshman comp class the previous day, these students weren't treating the tragedy as entertainment. Whether they were saddened or not, the mere proximity of death must have been sobering.

I couldn't help but wonder what she would think if she were looking in. Were those the characteristics by which people hoped to be remembered? These were essentially the same descriptors I had used myself, but did they sum up the person she was for over nineteen years of life? She told me she didn't really have friends. Had anyone known the true

Hadley? I wondered how her parents would have described her, or her siblings, if she had any.

Despite all of our talks after class and during office hours, I knew almost nothing about her background, what her family was like. I knew she took pills for anxiety and was a self-proclaimed introvert who was disappointed she didn't have many friends at college. I knew she had a job, but I didn't even know where. And I knew she had worked on the campus newspaper but had quit. When it came down to it, most of what I knew about Hadley was on the surface.

Then again, as her professor, I had access to a wealth of information: her essays. By this point in the semester, there had been only one lengthy paper, but I assigned a great deal of informal writing to train students in the habit of consistent literary analysis. The small papers helped students build up the skills and endurance the large ones required, just like a long-distance runner needed practice runs to be prepared for marathon day. And, though these were analytical essays, I also asked students to include a personal response at the bottom of each informal paper. Might Hadley have given anything away in one of these, some clue as to what was going on in her life? I'd have to check the online submission system and refresh my memory.

As I contemplated the real Hadley, whoever that was, my classroom had silenced. I jolted myself back to the present. Students had paid their respects and were waiting for my cue to see what came next.

Hadley's life mattered to this class, even if none of us knew her that well. Whether or not it would be appropriate to attend her funeral, whenever that information came out, I would have to decide later. But it was fitting to honor her here, to remember her in Grover Hall, where she had spent the last few weeks of her life for an hour and fifteen minutes every Monday and Wednesday evening.

"I know the syllabus states that we would discuss 'The Masque of the Red Death' today, and I'm assuming you've submitted your papers online. However, in light of what has happened, we're going to break form for once. It's not the right story for today. We'll get to that next class along with the story scheduled for Monday. For today, for Hadley, we'll read and analyze 'Annabel Lee,' which was *not* written in Pennsylvania as is our focus in this class, but it's about a young woman who perished before her time. This one, in particular, was published two days after Poe's death, and it's thought that he wrote it about his wife, Virginia. It's one of many where a narrator pines for a young woman who was taken too soon.

"I thought long and hard about how we should pay homage to our fallen classmate, and it seems right. For today. We'll read it quietly, then aloud, using different readers for each stanza, and then I'll ask you to jot down some initial reflections. More after we get to that part." I passed out copies of the poem.

With that, we began the humble task of honoring Hadley through the work of an author she loved. It was poignant, and beautiful in a way, but it didn't even start to make up for the fact that Hadley had died and no one knew what had happened to her.

I didn't like talking to those detectives, but if there was some morsel I could scrounge from her writing, some tidbit that could provide a clue, I would make it my mission to find and deliver it to them.

# Chapter 10

The next morning, Candace showed up again at my office door, her face blank. "Do you have a minute?"

I minimized my computer screen so she wouldn't see that I was looking back over Hadley's submitted work. "Sure."

"Dr. Lattimore called me this morning. He wanted me to let you know that Hadley's parents expressed their desire to meet with you. They're on campus right now, and I'm hoping you can make yourself available. I let Lattimore know that your class is over by 3:15."

I stared at her, unsure why the president of the university couldn't just call me himself. Why did he need to use Candace as a middleman?

"Okay. I mean, I'm willing to talk to them and express my condolences, but what should I *say* to them? And why me? I'm not a grief counselor, obviously, and I don't know what I can tell them that will help."

"Dr. Lattimore said they specifically requested you since Hadley had told them you were her favorite professor. He said that they were hoping to speak to some people who cared about their daughter and try to get an idea of what was going on in her life before she died." Candace sighed and massaged her temples. "I'm sorry to impose on you like this, Marissa. I know you don't have any answers for them. However, if the police find anything that leads back to Blackthorn University being implicated, it will go a long way that we were cooperative and kind to the parents."

"How would *Blackthorn* be implicated? I don't understand. What would the university possibly have to do with her death?"

"Historically, universities have been blamed and sued for all sorts of things. A student gets murdered and it's the university's fault that security wasn't better. A student commits suicide and the university can be held accountable for not seeing the warning signs and intervening. Even accidents have been taken to court—a student slips on ice, and it's the university's fault that the walkway wasn't cleared."

Candace shifted her weight; as department chair, I knew she was no stranger to the complicated world of campus politics. "Families often want to hold someone liable, so Dr. Lattimore wants to ensure we're all doing our parts to handle this situation just in case. He said to tell you how much he appreciates your cooperation, and that he'll certainly remember it."

I fought to keep my face impassive; Lattimore's method of *handling* Hadley's grieving parents made my skin crawl. This man had a message for me, what seemed like a thinly veiled bribe to maybe teach more classes after my contract ran out, but he didn't even call *me*; no, he sent Candace as his henchman to ensure I would act like a human being so the parents wouldn't sue. Even though I counted Candace on my miniscule list of friends, I didn't know how she felt about him, so I decided to hold back saying what I really thought. She was just following orders as department chair.

"*Of course* I'm willing to meet with them. Hadley was my

student, and I cared about her. I'll talk to them if that's what they want."

"Thank you, Marissa. They're meeting with Dr. Lattimore first, and I'll pass on the message that you'll be waiting for them at 3:30 in your office." She started to get up, having fulfilled her mission, but hesitated. "I know how this sounds, like it's all about staying out of court and not about the student. I'm sorry to have to talk about it this way, as if the parents are a time bomb ready to explode rather than two sad people mourning their only child. I've lost students, too, and it's awful. Trust me, I know that all universities deal with student deaths, but it seems Blackthorn has dealt with more than most. Thank you for being so understanding."

Hadley was an only child. That made it even worse.

---

JITTERY THE REST of the day, my nerves tingled in anticipation of the meeting. What would they ask me, and what would I *say*? It would be worse than meeting with the detectives—while they made me uncomfortable, I wasn't worried about saying the wrong thing, and I didn't care about *their* feelings. But how would I face this couple who had lost so much?

Staring at myself in the mirror, I practiced a look of concern. My face appeared to hold the appropriate level of distress, but I also noticed the dark circles under my eyes and deeper creases in my forehead. And was my hair falling out more than usual? Was Hadley's death or something else, a vestige of my own past trauma, affecting my body?

After class, back in my office, I perched on the edge of my chair, unable to use the time productively despite my nonstop flow of papers to grade and emails to answer. I kept an eye on the clock and urged it to move to quell my anxiety and get through this difficult meeting. I wanted to fast-forward to the end of it, but I owed these people my time if it would comfort them in some way.

I heard them in the hallway, their steps tentative as they searched for the correct office. If Lattimore himself couldn't guide them here, why not send someone else? But I knew the answer: If there's one thing I learned during my own heartbreak, it's that people are discomfited by the sadness of others. They think of it as a pestilence that might reach out with its cruel, searching fingers and pull them in, tainting their happiness.

"Dr. Owens?" Hadley's father, a tall, wiry man with the same startling blue eyes as Hadley—*eyes that would never see again*—held out his hand to mine.

"Hi. Yes. Please, sit down." I waited for them to get settled after my stilted opening, noticing the slowness of their movements, the delicate way in which they carried themselves, as if they needed to be careful not to break. "Let me just start by saying that I am so, so sorry for your loss."

"Thank you," Hadley's mother said. A small woman, everything about her seemed gray: her hair—although she didn't look much older than her mid-fifties—skin, and clothing, as if the color had been leached out of her, and I couldn't help but wonder how she had appeared before receiving the news that destroyed her world.

"We hope we're not imposing. I'm sure you're busy. It's been such a shock for us, and we wanted to come here and walk where Hadley walked and look at the trees and buildings she saw and breathe the air she breathed and talk to someone she trusted." The words came out in a rush, and then Hadley's mother seemed to close in on herself, buttoning up her lips and compressing into something smaller.

"It's no trouble." My wall clock ticked in the awkward

silence, and the moment stretched on as we stared at each other, none of us knowing how to proceed.

Hadley's father cleared his throat. "Can you tell us a little about Hadley, what she was like as a student? I don't mean her grades—I know she was getting an A in your class. She told me, and she was so proud. I mean, more like what was your experience with her, like did you know her well? She said she would talk to you sometimes, but I don't know if she meant really *talk* to you or just get help with her homework or something. She was always so quiet and shy that it was hard to know what was going on inside that big brain of hers. Even as a little girl, she wasn't chatty. I'd write down ideas of things we could talk about to get her going. I wanted to connect with her, but it was hard, and she never really had many friends, and no one's come forward except her roommate who didn't know her all that well, and now she's gone and all I want is to understand her more." His voice cracked.

He was all over the place, but I think I understood what he wanted: confirmation that Hadley had existed in this space and was noticed, appreciated. I could bestow him with that.

"Hadley was eager to come to class every day. She was thoughtful in her papers, providing insights and expressing her ideas in such a way that I always enjoyed reading hers."

It was true—I always graded alphabetically by last name, since that's how the papers appeared in the learning management system, and it was a relief when I reached Hadley's; I knew that I'd be reading something that didn't make me want to tear my hair out in frustration of another student half-assing their assignment or completing it last minute.

"We talked about her in class yesterday, and her classmates shared so many beautiful recollections." I repeated their stories and told them how we read the poem.

I watched as Mr. Parker put his arm around his wife, who was now emitting tiny sobs and shaking in her chair.

"Thank you, Dr. Owens. That means so much to us," she managed, her words low and husky.

"Please, call me Marissa." And then I blurted it out, the most personal thing about me, the tragedy I held in my heart: "I lost my child, too. My baby. A girl. She never lived, not outside of me. She was fine and then I went into labor and then her heartbeat became irregular, so I had emergency surgery, but we lost her. She died."

I pictured her tiny fingers, her cap of dark hair, those little legs that would never kick a soccer ball. I had felt the weight of her in my arms, little more than a bag of flour, before they took her from me. I didn't want to let her go, but David held me back while the doctor pried her away. They said it was time, but it wasn't. She was my little girl, my special person for whom I had waited for so long, through the years of not getting pregnant and the miscarriages. Each one seemed tragic at the time, but I hadn't even announced any of those pregnancies; they were all so early I didn't want to jinx them.

But with Emma—I named her Emma, Emma Rose, my perfect little flower—I had enjoyed a happy, healthy pregnancy. We had decorated the nursery in pinks and greens with her name painted on the wall in animal letters and bought all the little girl outfits for which we had yearned. We had gone overboard only in the last month of pregnancy, when we finally allowed ourselves to believe that *this* was the baby who would live.

But she died, right at the finish line, due to the umbilical cord being compressed. She was deprived of oxygen for too long. She suffocated before they could remove her from me.

My C-section scar seemed to throb at the memory. Since the wound had become infected and needed to be reopened for proper healing, the scar tissue developed into a thick, ropy line on my abdomen. I was glad it was there—proof my Emma had existed. Poe once wrote, "Never to suffer would never to have been blessed." I *was* blessed with Emma's brief time in my life, but the suffering continued to sting.

But these virtual strangers didn't need to know all this. "I'm sorry. I don't know why I told you that. It's not the same at all. My daughter's death was a tragedy, but it was a medical complication, not a mystery, and I didn't know her the way you knew your daughter." The words kept spilling out, tangling up in my mouth, and landing all wrong. This was *not* about me.

I felt Hadley's mother's hand in my own. She had reached across the desk to clasp it. I squeezed back, two mothers comforting each other.

We talked for a few more minutes, the Parkers telling me some stories about Hadley when she was growing up. They invited me to the funeral in York the following Tuesday and asked me to read "Annabel Lee." I agreed, and I watched them walk out of my office, hunched down like a much older couple.

My heart ached for them. A petty, mean part of me thought about how much luckier they were than I was—they had more than nineteen years with their daughter. And another part of me felt guilty because I didn't tell them what I had found, the clue I discovered lurking in an essay.

## CHAPTER 11

I dreamt of Emma that night. She was about four years old, the age she would have been if she'd lived. Since her death, Emma had appeared in my dreams sporadically; sometimes she was the tiny baby I had held, while other times she was growing in this parallel universe where she hadn't died. Sometimes David and I were married, and sometimes we weren't.

When I was in a dark place, I would think of these other worlds and long to trade places. Would David and I have stayed together if Emma had lived? Might we have even tried for another baby? In the real world, that was never an option, not after my emergency C-section caused endometriosis and made me, for all intents and purposes, infertile. I was willing to try again, but David said no, that we needed to grieve Emma properly. By then, I was forty with my child-bearing window rapidly diminished.

My sweet little Emma. Her looks changed as well as her age in my various dreams; she was blonde like David or brunette like me, her hair straight or curly. Though she was dark-haired at birth, it was hard to say what she might have looked like as

The nurses had given me a lock of her fine, silky hair after her tiny body was taken away. I kept it in a bag and took it out to stroke sometimes, but I only allowed myself that pleasure every few months. I was afraid it would fall apart, just dissolve, and I'd be left with nothing, just the cremains and the couple of photographs the hospital took for me, those sad, morbid pictures that reminded me of the portrait Poe had had painted of his wife, Virginia, after she died, the only known capture of her likeness.

That night, in my dream, Emma reached her hand out to me and said, "Mommy, you have to tell. Tell them. You need to help her."

Then it was Hadley standing there, saying, "You have to tell them, Dr. Owens."

When I woke up, those words were as clear in my head as if spoken in the real world. Whether it was my conscience telling me or not, I did what I didn't want to do. I took out Detective Ruiz's card and gave him a call.

"Ruiz," he answered, his voice terse and professional.

"It's Marissa Owens, Hadley Parker's professor. I may have found something important, but I'm not sure. I thought I should share it with you just in case." I decided to leave out that my dead daughter and Hadley herself had urged me to contact him in a dream.

"Good call. Are you at work or home? I can reach either address in about fifteen minutes."

I hadn't told him where I lived, but he was a detective, after all. "Can't I just tell you on the phone?" I hadn't showered yet and was still in my pajamas.

"I'd rather speak with you in person. Or you could come down to the station if you prefer?"

"I'm at home. You can come here, I guess." I didn't love the idea, and fifteen minutes didn't give me time to fully get ready for my day, but I could at least brush my teeth and put on a bra.

I hadn't had a single guest over since I'd moved into the apartment, not even Candace, and it unsettled me that the first person who would see my spartan, impersonal new home was a police detective, maybe two if Ruiz brought his partner.

Despite the non-friendly nature of this visit, I busied myself putting away the dishes in the draining tray and straightening my printouts on the kitchen table.

A sharp knock on my door announced Ruiz's presence.

"Good morning, Dr. Owens." Even though it was only seven a.m., he was dressed in a slim-fitting gray suit, whereas I had upgraded my jammies only slightly to my new Blackthorn hoodie and sweatpants. As soon as I saw him, I regretted not at least changing into jeans. Could someone in sweatpants be taken seriously?

Gesturing for him to sit down at the table, I noticed him taking in the stark contents of my apartment: no personal photographs on the wall, only a few framed art pieces, the secondhand furniture, the bookcase. "Dog?" he asked, pointing at the water bowl.

"Cat," I replied as Norman made his appearance, skittering across the floor and hissing at the intruder.

"I hate cats," Ruiz said, punctuating this statement with a sneeze. "Allergic."

"I'll put him in the bedroom."

When I returned, much to my annoyance, Ruiz was already looking at the printouts. "Is this what you wanted to show me? What am I looking at? This isn't even Hadley's paper."

"Yes, but Hadley was the peer reviewer for that student's paper." I had pored through everything she had turned in, just in case. But, even in those personal sections where she reacted to one of Poe's stories or a critical piece on his work, she hadn't given much away about her life that seemed relevant: She had written about her grandmother's funeral at one point, and she had made comparisons between Poe's work and some modern TV show that she enjoyed but I'd never heard of. I didn't know what I'd been looking for when I started rereading her essays, and I nearly missed what I *had* found, not on one of her own papers but on another student's.

"Before they turn in their bigger essays, I make them print out their rough drafts and bring them to class so they can give each other feedback. The one student reads their essay aloud to two peer reviewers who listen and make notes while the writer is reading, and then they talk about the essay."

Ruiz's dead stare made me think I needed to spend less time explaining my pedagogy and get to the point.

"So, the writer walks away with the hard copies of their essays with peer feedback, but they scan and upload this rough draft electronically to show they've gone through the writing process. I didn't think of it at first, but after I reread all of Hadley's writing to see if there were any cries for help or something that I'd missed, I thought I'd see what she wrote on her peers' essays. I looked at her files to see who had peer-reviewed her essay, and then I looked at those students' uploads to see what she wrote on their papers."

"And? What did you find?" Whether he was annoyed at my lengthy explanation or impressed by my thoroughness, I couldn't tell.

"Students don't just write comments on these drafts. While they're listening to the author read, they draw doodles, too. Look what Hadley wrote on this student's paper."

He leaned in to see the big reveal. "What are those—Greek letters?"

"Yes. Psi Omega Phi Phi. Don't you see what that means? If Hadley was writing those letters, she must have been pledging a sorority. I've seen it. Hell, I even did it myself.

Students become obsessed with getting in. They write the letters in secret while they're in class because pledging starts consuming them, and they think about it even when they're supposed to be doing other things."

Ruiz rubbed his eyes. Maybe he wasn't getting enough sleep working on this case, or maybe it was Norman's effect on his allergies. "It might not mean anything, necessarily, but it's something we'll follow up on since we've found zero evidence of this girl having any friends. Also, it would have been helpful to know that you took it upon yourself to meet with the parents of the deceased girl."

My face flushed. I felt like I was at the principal's office even in the sanctuary of my apartment. "They *asked* to meet with me. The president of the university had my department chair come talk to me and ask me to be nice to them. I was following orders and being a genuine human."

Seemingly appeased, he got out his notebook and appeared to copy down the Greek letters Hadley had written. "Do you know about this organization?"

"No, I don't know it. I googled the letters and couldn't find anything, not at Blackthorn and not nationally. And then it got me thinking: What if it's an underground sorority? What if they're not recognized by the university and keep everything secret?"

"Would you know anything about that, Dr. Owens? Underground sororities?" Ruiz asked, meeting my eyes, probing.

"I know that colleges have clamped down on Greek life. Things were different way back when, and now there are a bunch more regulations, which is good, but it's caused some organizations to disaffiliate themselves from universities entirely, so now there's no regulation, and they can do whatever they want."

*Tread carefully*, I warned myself.

"Let me get this straight. You're telling me you think Hadley was, what, pledging a secret underground sorority that's not recognized by the school, and somehow this is responsible for her death?"

"Detective, I'm just throwing it out there. I have no *idea* what happened to her, but I thought this information could be useful. I'm sorry if I wasted your time." I started gathering the papers up in a pile, frustrated. Wasn't this why Ruiz had given me his card?

He shot out his hand and stopped me, holding onto the paper. "I'll keep this if it's okay with you. We have very little to go on, and it may be helpful after all. I *do* want you to know that Hadley Parker's death is an active investigation, so please do not share this information with anyone else, not your colleagues, not your students, not even Hadley's parents if you see them again. We have a Victim Support Coordinator working with the Parkers, and I can assure you that we are sharing relevant information with them."

I nodded to show I understood, although the desire to help grated against my annoyance that he thought he needed to warn me against running my mouth, as if this were just some hot gossip rather than a girl's life. "What *is* my role, then? Should I keep looking for clues?"

No sooner had these words escaped my lips than I realized how foolish I sounded, like I was planning to cruise around in the Mystery Machine with my trusty pooch, Scooby-Doo.

"Please do *not* look for clues. I appreciate that you want to help, but you need to leave the investigation to the professionals. In Pennsylvania, the Right-to-Know Law means that we'll disclose the manner of the victim's death to the public, but other information needs to be held back to help us apprehend any suspect who may be involved." Ruiz was all by the book— he didn't display a flicker of irritation, nor did he seem sorry to keep me in the dark.

I persisted all the same. "Do you have a suspect in her death? Was it murder?"

"Some new information has come to light that will be revealed at a press conference today. That's all I can say for now."

He put away his notebook and rose from the table. Before he reached the door, he paused and turned around, as if he remembered some manners. "Thank you for contacting me. Try to go about your day and trust that the other police and I are doing our jobs. Hadley will receive justice."

Without another word, he was gone.

I had laid all my cards—just *about* all of them—on the table for him, but I came away from this interview with several questions. If he said that Hadley would receive justice, though, he was indicating that her death was *un*justified.

---

FINALLY, it was time for the press conference. I hurried back to my apartment after class to watch and write down anything important. Even though Ruiz said to leave matters to the police, I was invested. I wanted to know what happened to Hadley.

I turned on the local news station, where a bewildered-looking reporter in an ill-fitting sports jacket provided a few preliminary sentences before the camera moved to the empty podium and microphone set up in the front of the room. After an awkward minute or two of silence, a portly man with thinning gray hair walked up and cleared his throat.

"Good evening. I am Henry Rogers, Chief of Police. The information being released today is the result of the efforts of the Blackthorn Police Department. As you now know, nineteen-year-old Blackthorn University student Hadley Parker of York, Pennsylvania, was found deceased on Monday afternoon. Based on the decomposition of the body, the coroner estimates she died roughly eight days prior to being found. These results coordinate with her last known appearance."

The police chief paused, and the only sounds were the shuffling of people in the room and some muffled coughs. "I've raised my family in this town. My two daughters, now grown and moved away, were also students at Blackthorn University. As a father, as a member of this community, it gives me great pains to provide this next information, and my heart goes out to Mr. and Mrs. Parker."

He gestured, and the camera panned to the front row of chairs, where the Parkers huddled together. Mr. Parker, his face set in a grimace, straightened up at the sound of his name, while Mrs. Parker placed her head into her hands. They must have been previously informed of what would be presented.

A chill coursed through me as I waited. While getting the answers wouldn't bring Hadley back, I hoped her parents would gain closure by learning what happened.

"An examination of the body showed troubling signs. First, a blood screen detected both pregnancy hormones and the presence of Rohypnol, which is known by the street name of 'roofies,' also called the date rape drug. It is placed into a victim's drink to render the victim incapacitated."

Rogers hesitated again, giving the crowd a chance to process this information. He opened his mouth to continue but took an additional moment to pass his hand over his face, as if he needed to force out the vile words.

"Second, the autopsy revealed that the victim had been given an abortion, which was crudely and dangerously performed. The cause of death is blood loss. The victim bled out following the removal of the fetus, which was not recovered. The victim's blood was not found at the scene, verifying that the body was moved postmortem.

"As such, Ms. Parker was not alone when she died. If she

had self-administered the Rohypnol, it is unlikely that she could have performed the procedure and impossible that she would have been able to clean herself up, dispose of the fetus as well as the surgical implements, and move herself away from the site of the botched surgery. We don't know who did this to her, or why, but we are determined to find out. Someone may have taken her to the state park to make it look like an accident, but this death was not natural. Even if the victim wished to end the pregnancy and asked for help in doing so, what happened next is a crime."

Rogers gazed straight into the camera. "Hadley Parker's death was preventable. If someone, her assailant or anyone else who may have seen Ms. Parker in distress, had intervened and called 911, she would be alive. But she's dead. She is dead, and one or more persons are at fault. *Some*one sold or provided the assailant with that drug. *Some*one performed the abortion. *Some*one knows what happened to her, and we will get to the bottom of it. If you are sitting at home watching this press conference right now and know something that could bring the assailant to justice, please contact the Blackthorn Police Department.

"We are seeking the public's help. Hadley Parker was last reported seen by her roommate on the afternoon of Sunday, October 2, and last spoke with her parents that same day. If you saw Hadley Parker then or the next day, before she failed to respond to a text message from her mother and failed to attend her college classes on Monday, October 3, let us know. We believe she was already deceased by that day.

"If you saw her with someone that Sunday, *say* something. If you visited Water's Edge State Park and saw a car, or saw two people walking, one possibly holding the other up, *call* us. Hadley Parker did not own a car and did not drive there herself. Someone took her there and left her, living or already dead, alone in those woods.

"If there is someone watching right now who knows what happened, we urge you to come forward. If you are the person responsible for this tragedy, we will find you. Come to justice now before we apprehend you."

Hadley's picture filled the screen as Rogers continued speaking. It was a photo I hadn't seen before—perhaps her senior portrait from high school. Hadley looked younger and more innocent than in the flirty Facebook photos.

"This is Hadley Parker. It *was* Hadley Parker, since someone caused the actions, on purpose or not, that extinguished her life. May you rest in peace, Hadley, and may God grant the Blackthorn Police Department the means to find your killer."

I turned off the TV and stared at my notes, speechless. I didn't know what I was expecting to be revealed, but it wasn't *that*. Someone had drugged her, performed an unsafe abortion, and allowed her to die rather than risking exposure of their crime. And they left her body in the woods to rot, the way one might leave a discarded jack-o-lantern after Halloween.

*Rohypnol. Abortion. Blood loss. Killer.* These words swam around my head, unwelcome visitors, as I tried to fall asleep.

## CHAPTER 12

### THEN

**M**arissa ended up rooming with a stranger during sophomore year and planned to remain distant from her. If she opened up, if she let people in, they always ended up disappointing her. They would choose others over her, and could she blame them? She wanted to believe she was worthy of friendship, but she had no evidence of that. She should have gotten used to it by now.

It wasn't anyone's fault, not really. Everyone seemed nice enough, but could she really trust someone after being let down so many times? She had reached out to Amber over the summer vacation once, and they had a pleasant conversation, if a little more formal than in the past, but Amber hadn't asked Marissa to hang out since they'd been back at college. And her former roommate, Scarlett, sweet girl that she was, always had plans with her sorority. She had asked Marissa to join her at a party, and Marissa complied, but she felt out of place amongst all the Greek letters emblazoned on everyone's chests.

No, she would keep to herself this year. She requested additional hours at the library and threw herself into he studies during the first few weeks of sophomore year. She would focus on her education, not her social life. By getting a degree, she would ensure her future. She didn't need popularity to be successful in college.

But a chance meeting changed everything. Having completed a challenging exam in biology class, Marissa treated herself to a piece of cake and a latte at the local diner. She squirreled her savings away, normally, but wanted a little pick-me-up in her rigid, quiet life. She permitted herself this luxury, reading a book for pleasure and enjoying the indulgence.

Marissa smiled as she took in her surroundings: the black and white checkered floor, the gleaming glass pastry display cabinet, the friendly waitresses with their pink, logo-bearing shirts. Everything and everyone looked clean and shiny. She felt relaxed and content in her own space, by herself, as the diner buzzed around her.

"Hey, do you mind if I sit with you? It's packed in here." A girl's voice brought her back from her thoughts.

*No, tell her no*, Marissa thought, but she didn't want to be rude. Maybe they could sit together in silence, each in their own space. "Sure, okay." She forced a smile and moved her backpack—purposely placed to indicate that she was here alone, of her own volition—from the bench across from her.

"I think we're in the same biology class, right? I'm Kai. Do you have Osborn? Did you just take that exam?"

"Yeah, I did. That's why I'm here, to let off some steam and enjoy some downtime." Marissa left off the words "alone time" so as not to offend. Marissa recognized Kai from class, and she seemed harmless and nice enough. She always attended and even raised her hand to participate sometimes, an act that was allowed on rare occasions in the dry, lecture-heavy course.

"I think I bombed it, even after studying all night! Can

you see these bags under my eyes? I could pack some luggage in here! How do you think you did?"

"I studied a lot, too, and I think I did well on the multiple-choice questions, but I got stuck on some of the short answers."

Despite everything, Marissa found herself relaxing in Kai's company, talking about school, movies, music, and books. Kai was a Stephen King fan, too, she said, and she'd already read *Needful Things*, the very book Marissa had brought to the diner. *And* she also loved the Red Hot Chili Peppers, which she shared after spotting the patch on Marissa's backpack.

Kai was a bit odd—who goes to a diner by themselves and sits down with a stranger? She was kind of alternative-looking, with a purple streak in her blonde hair, thrift store-looking clothes that made her look cool rather than poor, and Doc Martens boots. But she was funny and sweet and utterly unselfconscious, telling Marissa all about her life in Bangor, Maine—just like Stephen King! She didn't know him and also didn't say "ayuh" like many of his characters, but she admitted to busting out with an occasional "wicked" at times when excited.

"So, not to be weird—oops, sorry, probably too late for that—do you want to hang out again? Maybe we could be study buddies and get ready for our next biology test?" Kai asked, grinning.

"I'd like that," Marissa said, and she meant it. For all Kai's bubbliness, maybe she needed a friend, too, and they seemed to click. They exchanged phone numbers, and Marissa hoped Kai would reach out, that this was a real connection.

———

AND IT WAS. Kai sat by her in the next biology class, and they suffered together through Dr. Osborne's droning lecture.

While Marissa never skipped class, she dreaded the boring ones, but now she looked forward to Kai's whispered jokes and goofy drawings of their professor. Marissa had to stifle a laugh a few times due to Kai's antics, but she didn't mind, and Dr. Osborne couldn't be bothered to pay attention to what any of his students were doing anyway. If he didn't notice the snoring of the guy who sat behind her every class, surely he wouldn't notice the tiny bit of off-task behavior Marissa had started to demonstrate. She still turned in all her work and gave her best effort.

Despite the easy in-class comradery, Marissa continued to hold back somewhat, having been burned too often by female friendships that glowed so bright but flickered out with lightning speed. She didn't push it, ever—she never asked Kai if she wanted to hang out. She waited for her new friend to initiate everything, worried she'd come on too strong and ruin this delicate connection. It had happened before.

But Kai *kept* wanting to hang out, persisted in asking Marissa to go to parties with her and her roommate or come over to her dorm room to watch a movie. When the day came that Kai told her she wanted to pledge a sorority, and said that she should, too, Marissa explained her hesitation.

"I went through rush last year, and it wasn't for me. My roommate pledged Tri Pi, and I really like her, but I don't know that I want to be a part of something like that." Marissa didn't want to disappoint Kai, but she also didn't want to set herself up for rejection—again.

"No duh, rush sucks! I didn't even go since I heard it was so lame. Are you kidding me with the freakin' cucumber sandwiches, like we're the Queen of England or something? But, you know Hannah, that girl who's friends with my roommate Jessica? She said that there's an alternative way to pledge where you don't need deal with that fake bullshit. It's called COB, Continuous Open Bidding. It's where a sorority can do an informal thing and just be real, and if you're a good match for each other, it works, and they give you a bid, and you accept it."

"But I don't know that I *want* to be in a sorority, Kai. Rush made me feel like the sororities were judging me, like I wasn't good enough, and I hate that." Marissa knew Kai enough by now that she felt comfortable sharing some of her insecurities. "And which sorority do you even want to pledge? Because most of them didn't offer me bids last spring, and I doubt that anything's different now. It's not like I'm suddenly better looking or cooler now than I was then."

Marissa pointed to herself, touching her hair which didn't quite fit the sorority girl mold, her outfit that wasn't stylish enough even though she kept trying to figure out fashion. Those sorority girls seemed effortlessly glamourous—and exclusive. Even for Kai, Marissa didn't want to put herself out there like that again.

"Look, I'm not trying to twist your arm that much, but I've met a bunch of girls in Omega Kappa Beta, and they're awesome. They're not like the other sororities. For one, they're a local sorority, not national, so there's no bigger organization overseeing them to tell them how to act or collect crazy dues. Didn't you meet them at rush? Some are hippie chicks, some are athletes, and some really care about school and their grades like you! And it will be so much better if we pledge together! Jessica's great, but I just feel more *comfortable* with you. We could do this together and find our tribe."

*Our tribe.* This was why Kai and Marissa were friends. Kai wanted it, too, that feeling that she belonged. Marissa thought back to rush. With fifteen sororities on campus competing for pledges, some of the visits were less memorable than others. OKB seemed laid back and cool with their beach theme and Bob Marley music, but they hadn't given that same sense of allure and privilege she had felt at Sig Om. She had *liked* OKB, but she hadn't yearned to be a part of them. Maybe that's what she got wrong before.

"Kai, I'm nervous. What if they don't like me?"

"We're in this together. If we don't like their vibe, or if they don't like ours, forget it. We only do this if it feels right. I promise."

---

A DINGY BUILDING with peeling wallpaper and the lingering odor of stale cigarette smoke and cheap beer, the sorority house where OKB held their event was a far cry from Sig Om's regal brownstone. Marissa walked in with her small group—Kai, Kai's roommate Jessica, and Jessica's friend Hannah. A few other non-sorority girls sat on threadbare couches nibbling pretzels or Cheez-Its from bowls on a table. The sisters, identifiable by their matching tie-dyed OKB shirts, milled about the room chatting with each other, laughing, and making small talk with the visiting girls, some of whom they seemed to know.

A tall, slim girl with a mass of curly brown hair called for attention, and the murmurings ceased. "My name is Danielle, and I'm the president of Omega Kappa Beta. First, I'd like to welcome you all to our house. Thank you for coming and providing us with the opportunity to tell you about our sorority. Second, we want to show you who we really are—not that pretentious BS you might get from some of the cookie-cutter sororities. I'm friends with many of them, and they're wonderful girls, but where they value conformity and have rules for how to act and dress, we are multi-faceted. We come from different backgrounds, have different strengths and weaknesses, and look different than each other. Some of us are most comfortable going to class in sweatpants, and some of us"—she gestured to a voluptuous girl in heels and full makeup—"like to glam it up. We allow everyone to retain their uniqueness but are stronger together. We're there for each other through all the highs and lows, supporting each other to achieve our dreams."

Danielle introduced the other officers, each of whom offered a tidbit about the sorority as well as a personal story of how it was meaningful to them. They shared a video of various activities, intramural sports and bake sales and community service, where the girls all laughed and smiled. Afterward, they broke off into smaller groups of sisters and prospective pledges, running through icebreaker games. Though Kai and Marissa were split into separate groups, they caught each other's glances a few times and gave nods of encouragement.

Near the end of the evening, when the sisters left to confer in private about whom they would offer a bid, Marissa and the others waited with anticipation but not dread. It felt comfortable here. Kai squeezed Marissa's hand.

Danielle walked back into the room, grinning. "Ladies, we are so privileged to become acquainted with you this evening. This is a special group, truly unique. We would like to invite each of you to pledge Omega Kappa Beta, to enter into the journey to sisterhood. We will hand each of you a bid. If you accept, please sign your name and place the bid in the chalice. If you do not answer the call to sisterhood, we bear you no hard feelings, and we still hope to see you at one of our Thursday night happy hours."

Marissa signed her name on the bid, a simple rectangular printout.

# CHAPTER 13

Despite all the new information about Hadley's death, it was another routine day at Blackthorn that Monday. Students laughed and joked with each other before class, stared at their phones, complained about some professor or another, and talked about the upcoming football game. If my freshmen were bothered by the news, which I knew they had heard by then, I didn't see any evidence of it.

Following Friday afternoon's police announcement, President Lattimore waited until early Monday morning to send another email:

Dear Campus Community,

As you may have learned, the police released new information on Friday about the death of our student, Hadley Parker. We are saddened to learn how Hadley suffered before her death. Blackthorn University is fully cooperating in the investigation.

Although Hadley's death occurred off campus, your leadership team at Blackthorn University is committed to maintaining a safe, healthy college experience for our students. We are currently expanding outreach to inform our students of options if they become pregnant. We are looking for students to participate in the creation of this program and offer their voices.

If these events are triggering to you, please reach out to the Women's Center or Counseling Center. At Blackthorn University, we care about your feelings.

Sincerely,

Andrew Lattimore, Ph.D.

President, Blackthorn University

*Was* it sincere, or was it just lip service, placating the students and their parents so they didn't head for the hills, taking their tuition dollars with them? Actions mattered more than these words. Lattimore's unspoken concern in this PR nightmare was for an enrollment decline next year.

Why did he make it a point to say that the event occurred off campus? Was that so important? And why was there no mention of the Rohypnol? Hadley's unsafe abortion killed her, according to Chief Rogers, but the fact she was roofied had to be important, too. Did the baby's father drug her and try to take care of the unplanned pregnancy, abandoning her in the woods when it went south? Why would a college student—assuming that's who fathered the baby—possibly think he would know how to abort a fetus?

Whether or not Hadley consented to the abortion, someone had done it to her. Maybe she was an inconvenient woman whom someone believed they needed to silence. My male students seemed like nice enough guys, but statistics told me that I had most likely taught rapists and abusers in my classes over the years. Those same guys who smiled and said good morning and came from church-going families could sometimes turn villainous in other circumstances, slipping pills into girls' drinks at a bar or insisting on sex after a girl said no.

I closed my eyes and saw Hadley's face. And then another face popped into my head, another innocent girl who didn't deserve what had happened to her, a face I could picture as if I had seen her yesterday.

I couldn't go there. Opening my eyes, I banished that second girl to the depths of my memory and looked out at the students in front of me, focusing on people who were alive and well and hopefully not rapists or abusers. I had only two minutes before class started, and I needed to concentrate on the here and now. When my thoughts raced like this, threatening to boil over and consume me, I practiced a mental exercise to calm myself, taking stock of my present circumstances to come back into the moment.

*I am standing in my classroom. My shoes are pinching my feet. There are gray clouds in the sky. Chris has green hair now.*

Refocused, ready for class, I locked the vault on everything else in my head.

---

WHEN I HEADED BACK to my office, he was waiting, sitting on the vinyl couch near my door with one leg crossed at the knee, as casually as any student wanting to negotiate a grade on an essay. I caught a flash of argyle sock before he stood.

"Hello, Detective," I said.

"Dr. Owens, hello. I was hoping for a minute if you have one?" Ruiz wore a black suit today, slim cut like the others, and, for the first time, I got the sense that he was actually asking for my time rather than demanding it.

"Sure." I opened my office door, set down my bag, and sat, weary from this but curious. "No Welch today?"

"This isn't *official* police business, so no. I'm on my lunch break and wanted to stop by."

A tiny spot of mustard on his otherwise pristine white shirt indicated he'd already had a hasty bite. He looked at me, really stared from large brown eyes framed with thick lashes, his lips pursed in a tight line. "I assume you watched Friday's press conference."

"Yes, of course." I pictured the police chief's grim expression and remembered those haunting words: *We will find you.* How I hoped for those words to come true.

"It's all very upsetting." What an understatement.

"I wanted to see how you were doing." He held my gaze again.

I shrugged. "I don't know. She's not mine to mourn. I'm sad, and I feel awful for her, that her last moments must have been terrifying if she was aware of what was happening, and it's scary to think that someone, maybe even the baby's father, did this to her, and that they could be wandering around like nothing happened, not in custody or anything, while Hadley's probably at a funeral home by now, and who knows? Maybe they're a student here, sitting in class and writing papers and thinking they got away with it because they *did* get away with it, didn't they? They could have impregnated Hadley and left her to die, or at least didn't do anything to stop her from dying, and what, they just get to keep on going?" I said it all, rambling away before I realized how loud my voice had gotten.

"We do *not* want this person to get away with it, and I can assure you that we're doing everything within our power to prevent that from happening." He cleared his throat. "I was wondering if all this might be, ahh, triggering for you. That's why I wanted to check in on you today, see how you were doing."

I felt the heat rise in my face. "Triggering how?"

*And what do you know?* I wanted to add.

"Dr. Owens, I looked into you. We always check out the people we interview. Your name came up on an old witness list from when you were a student. I read your interview transcript."

"Right. Of course." I didn't know what else to say and didn't want to talk about it. I avoided his gaze but could feel his eyes on me. Time to change the subject.

"Did you find out anything about Psi Omega Phi Phi, the potential underground sorority Hadley might have been pledging? Anything you can tell me, anyway?"

"Not yet. I'm interviewing the Director of Greek Life later today. Rob Healy? You know him?"

I shook my head. "I don't really know *any*one. I stay to myself, do my work, that sort of thing. I've probably talked to you more than I've talked to any of my colleagues, except my one friend, my former professor who convinced me to apply here."

"That would be Candace Cabrera, the chair of the English Department, correct?" To my quizzical look, he responded, "I *told* you I looked into you." A smile played on the corner of his lips.

This was starting to feel very different from his so-called official police business. Time to put a fork in it. "If there's nothing else, Detective, I really should get back to work. I have grading to do, and I don't want to keep you from catching your killer."

"Right." He got up and gave me a little salute. "Nice to see you again, Marissa."

"Nice to see you, too."

He left me to my grading.

*He called me Marissa.*

LATER THAT NIGHT, Hadley's death having distracted me from my rule of being prepared in advance, I realized I hadn't made my copies for the next day—the citation 911 handout I had created to help my freshmen. While this shouldn't have been a source of stress, as the copier was reliable and rarely had a huge line, it was one more item to accomplish on a long list of tasks.

Sighing, I hauled myself off the couch and grabbed my jacket and purse. At ten p.m., no one would be around to see me in my Adidas flip-flops and sweatpants, so I didn't bother changing. It would be a quick trip in and out of the office, and taking care of the chore would make me sleep better that night.

I pulled into the empty parking lot outside of Willis Center. Dull halos of illumination surrounded the streetlights, providing respite from complete blackness, but it felt *too* dark, quiet, and desolate as I walked the short distance to the entrance. Looking to the left and right, I scanned for movement and could have sworn I heard a rustling, but it was probably the October wind.

After I scanned my ID, the lock clicked open, and I rushed to close the door behind me. *I should've waited until the morning*, I thought, but I was there now, and it would be a waste not to complete my mission. I was fine. I was *safe*. Whoever had killed Hadley had no interest in hurting or stalking me. I was acting like a little girl afraid of the dark.

I went about my business, listening to the grating yet rhythmic sounds of the copier and chiding myself for feeling panicked. Still, I was anxious to leave. After dropping off the copies in my office, I decided to take the stairwell as a shortcut on my way out.

With my office all the way up on the third floor, I had to descend two flights of stairs to reach the hub of the English department or any exit. Even though Willis Center was one of

Blackthorn's newer buildings, the stairwell reminded me of a secret passageway in an old mansion with its out-of-the-way access points and minimal lighting—a few sconces spaced far apart and kept on low.

After closing the heavy door, I hurried down the unadorned concrete stairs, conscious not to trip on my flip-flops. All I needed was to end up falling with no one to help me. The clatter of my quick steps echoed up the cinder block walls to the cavernous ceiling.

Then I heard a distinct click, like the gentle closing of a door. My heart pounding, I looked upward but didn't see anyone. Pausing my stride, I strained to hear footsteps other than my own.

Nothing. *Of course* there was nothing. I was by myself in a building that required identification to enter. Only the professors or staff members with offices here—along with the custodial crew—could gain access outside of workday hours. Maybe that sound was the heating system. Nonetheless, I hurried down the remaining stairs and jogged to my car, my blood rushing in my ears and my palms sweating. I locked the doors and drove home.

I was being silly.

Wasn't I?

No one was after me.

I was fine.

Everything was fine.

## CHAPTER 14

### THEN

What is the tipping point from reasonable and normal to unacceptable and toxic? Marissa wasn't sure when it happened for her. It seemed fun at first, just what she wanted: She belonged to a group. Not the sorority, not yet, but being a part of OKB's Fall 1998 pledge class felt like something big, something special, in a life that had been too quiet and solitary in the past several months. Although she didn't feel close with any of the pledges other than Kai at first, there was the shared circumstance that bonded them, not to mention safety in numbers.

They started with a pledge class of seven but lost two almost immediately, well before anything demanding had happened. Sammi and Kristen didn't tell anyone they were thinking about dropping, but then they didn't show up to the second meeting, and that was that. They left their red and black metal pledge pins engraved with the sorority letters in the OKB house's mailbox.

In the beginning, pledging was barely more of a change to their schedules than any other extracurricular activity, like Math League or cross country had been for Marissa back in high school. OKB wanted the pledges to take school seriously so they could transition into active sisters upon initiation and not flunk out; thus, they required mandatory three-hour study halls Sunday through Thursday nights. None of the other pledges had jobs, but Marissa had to finagle her hours so that they wouldn't interfere with her pledging schedule. It helped that her supervisor at the library was understanding to the point of embarrassment.

"I'm so happy to hear that you're pledging a sorority!" Mrs. Reinhart had actually *clapped her hands*. "It's good for young girls to find a group. And you'll make lifelong friends, maybe even find a boyfriend! That's how I met Mr. Reinhart —in college at a fraternity/sorority mixer!"

Marissa couldn't picture the kaftan-wearing, bespectacled, grandmother-like woman as a young and flirty student, nor did she want to, but she appreciated her boss's flexibility.

The sorority was less understanding. Marissa talked to Angela, the assistant pledge mistress, who had just pledged last semester and was also a sophomore, about the quandary. Her time was limited, and she needed to fulfill her twenty hours at circulation services, checking out library books and materials. Marissa had been upfront about her need to work from the time she had accepted her bid, and the sisters were quick to say that having a job was acceptable as long as it wouldn't interfere with her pledging responsibilities.

Angela was sweet. "I have to work, too, and I worked when I was pledging." She glanced around before adding, "Some of the girls come from different backgrounds than us, but I'm poor, too."

Marissa's cheeks flamed at this uncomfortable recognition, but at least Angela could relate. She wondered what had given her away as coming from poverty, but she didn't ask.

Since Marissa's work hours had been predetermined during that first week of pledging, and since she hadn't decided to sign the bid until minutes in advance, she didn't have enough time to get a shift replacement. She didn't like it, but she had to miss her very first sorority function that Monday night.

If Marissa had been forced to choose between pledging and work, she would have had to keep her job; she needed the money, no question, or she wouldn't be able to stay in college. But ever since she had signed her name, Marissa was plagued with anxiety about her decision to pledge: fears that the sorority would find out how uncool she truly was and kick her out, or that pledging would interfere with her schoolwork, or even that her one true friend, Kai, would tire of her.

As it turned out, what she missed was the naming function. According to Kai, who clued Marissa in later that night over the phone, all the pledges had to tell an embarrassing story about themselves. Then, the sisters picked a pledge name for them based on the story or some aspect of their personality. This was pretty much what her roommate Scarlett had told her had happened in Tri Pi, one of the last times she had shared anything about the inner workings of sorority life before she clammed up, refusing to divulge "secrets of the sisterhood."

Kai had whispered into the phone even though her roommate, Jessica, was also pledging and had heard it all firsthand. "I don't know why, but I told them about when I got caught shoplifting in high school. I stole a bottle of nail polish from the drug store, just a dumb and impulsive thing, and they put my photo up and I couldn't go there for two years. They never called the cops, thank God, but it was incredibly mortifying, and my parents practically disowned me. And now I'm Pledge Klepto. And everyone at Blackthorn will know I did something stupid!" Kai's voice, heavy with regret, stuck in her throat.

"Are you okay? Do you want to ask them to change it?

They seemed pretty understanding about me having to miss tonight, as long as I don't do it again." Marissa yearned for exoneration—a rule follower, she avoided trouble. She had gone her whole life this way, never skipping class or receiving detention, never talking back to a teacher or adult in charge.

"No, it's my fault. I just drew a blank when they said to tell something embarrassing. That was downright *humiliating*. We still don't talk about it in my family. Everyone else came up with something cute or funny, like about how they got caught making out under the bleachers or burped when they gave a speech or something, and I came up with *that*."

Kai sighed. "I feel like such a dumbass."

"I'm sorry, Kai. I bet lots of people have done stuff like that, so you just need to act like it doesn't bother you, even if it does." After waiting a respectful beat, Marissa finally allowed herself to ask what she had been dying to know. "Since I wasn't there, will they do mine later?"

Her brain on overdrive, Marissa cataloged her many, many awkward experiences and tried to summon one that was funny rather than terrible. There was that time she was working as a lifeguard at the waterpark and forgot to put her shirt and shorts on before heading to the company picnic at which she was the only one wearing just a swimming suit... it had been super uncomfortable walking around in that blue one-piece when everyone else was clothed, but she pretended it didn't bother her. Pledge Swimsuit? Too obvious and not at all clever.

"Marissa, they *named* you already. They said you should have been there but weren't. You're Pledge Fugitive."

"But I *told* them I had to work. They said it was okay as long as I didn't miss another one." Marissa's words rushed out, her pulse quickening. "Am I in trouble already? Is this okay?"

"I think it's fine. It's early days, and they wouldn't have

given you a bid if they didn't want you to become a sister someday." Kai's tone was still off. Wasn't pledging supposed to be fun? They were already both upset by the first full day. "But, anyway, we'll have a meeting tomorrow after our study hall. Apparently, we're gonna design our pledge books, so bring markers and shit. Or puffy paint if you have that."

"What the hell is puffy paint?"

"No freakin' idea. They just said 'puffy paint' like we'd know, and I didn't want to ask. I got myself in enough trouble just telling my story."

"Kai, are we doing the right thing? Should we actually be doing this? You don't sound happy, and it's not too late to turn back. We barely started."

"No, Marissa. It's not that. I just screwed up. I shouldn't've said what I said, but it was still fun, like with a lot of bonding with the sisters, and they even told us about some of their names." She snort-laughed, the most positive sound Marissa had heard since they got on the phone.

"Like what?" Marissa was eager for some levity, anxious to break the tension from their own unfortunate pledge names.

"One girl—Maribeth, if you remember her? Kind of short with dark hair and bangs? Well, she peed her pants in first grade since her dad terrified her about germs in public toilets. But it was raining, and she leaned up against the bricks so the whole back of her pants got wet, and she got away with it!"

"And her pledge name was...?"

"Sneaky Pee! It was really funny how she told it. We were practically crying." Marissa could hear the smile in her friend's voice.

"Kai, I think we'll be okay. We're in this together, right?"

"You bet. Forever friends."

They said goodbye and hung up. Marissa looked through her desk drawer and found her markers. She would make this work. She *so* wanted to make this work, even if she had to respond to the name Pledge Fugitive.

---

*IT WAS FINE*, Marissa told herself afterward. *They like you. You fit in.*

Mrs. Reinhart had given Marissa a huge—and humiliating—wink when she and her four pledge sisters, having met outside five minutes before the study hall started, trudged into the library together, single file.

Not everyone was as studious as she, Marissa soon learned. Having entrenched herself in a cubicle, she opened her immense British Literature I tome and got to work. Hannah and Janelle, two of the other girls, couldn't stop giggling, and that would have been fine if Marissa wasn't trying to concentrate on *The Canterbury Tales*, but she was. If she could focus on her schoolwork at the library, she'd have the mental space to attend to the pledging stuff later.

Just as she was underlining a passage in her book, Hannah let out a particularly loud guffaw, and Marissa's pen scribbled across the page. The discordant sound also brought out Jasper, a hunched, grizzled Vietnam vet, from behind the desk.

He surveyed the small group with a snarl on his face. "If you girls don't quieten down, I'm kicking you outta here."

The girls exchanged a look, and even Hannah and Janelle froze. They *had* to be here; it was a requirement of pledging. Every half hour or so, some sister or other would come check on them, and if they weren't studying...

While she, too, wanted some peace and quiet, a rage bubbled up inside Marissa at the audacity of this man telling them what to do. It wasn't part of the job description for the student workers to patrol the library and police the students. This was the same man who, just a couple of weeks ago, had yelled at her for not reshelving all the books that had been returned even though her shift had ended and Mrs. Reinhart told the employees not to work beyond their scheduled time. Despite the fact that this man was an undergraduate student, like her, Marissa had cowered when he had confronted her, barely able to stammer out her apology.

But she wasn't letting that happen again, not in front of her pledge sisters. She stood up. "Jasper, we have every right to be here, and we don't answer to you. Go back to the desk and do your actual *job*."

Jasper's furor painted itself upon his face, red and ugly, and he walked closer, pointing his finger at her. "I don't answer to you, girl! Just shut the fuck up!" But he walked away all the same.

"Wow, Marissa, thanks," Janelle said, bestowing her with a toothy, if shaky, smile. "That was awesome. That guy seems super scary. You got us all out of trouble."

"He's a bully," was all Marissa said, but everyone settled down after that, and she got back to work in blissful quiet, her skin tingling for having stood up to someone for once.

---

LATER, at the OKB house, they designed their pledge books, simple three-subject notebooks decorated with Greek letters cut from construction paper. Jessica, now known as Pledge Grenade, an art major, drew outlines of their pledge names in fancy lettering that they colored in with magic markers. Some of the more artistic sisters joined in by contributing doodles of their favorite OKB elements: the flower (pansy), the mascot (trident), and the gem (garnet, to go along with the sorority colors of red and black).

Marissa didn't enjoy filling in the letters of her cringe-worthy new name, Pledge Fugitive, but she loved the easy comradery of the group and the new respect she had earned after the situation with Jasper. No one mentioned her absence the previous night, even though she noticed that the sisters only referred to her, and the other newbies, by their pledge names.

There was some eighties mix playing on the CD player, and the few sisters in the room whooped with delight when Bon Jovi's "Livin' on a Prayer" came on.

Angela, the assistant pledge mistress, explained, "It's our sorority song," before joining the rest in a raucous display while the pledges looked on.

Marissa smiled at seeing tiny, timid Angela so animated and happy along with confident, statuesque Danielle and glamorous Bianca. These girls were so different from each other, yet they were bonded together by their sisterhood in a way that other friends weren't. She looked across the living room at Kai and knew that they had made the right choice.

---

DECORATING the pledge book was step one. The next night at their pledge meeting, this time run by the pledge mistress herself, Courtney, they learned why the books were so important.

Marissa hadn't seen much of Courtney until that night, and she was all business, speaking with that overly formal language many of the sisters used when discussing rules and traditions. Unlike the others, though, Courtney *always* spoke properly, avoiding the slang and profanity to which Marissa was accustomed.

"Your pledge book is your lifeline to becoming a part of the sisterhood and must remain with you at all times," Courtney explained, her voice filling the small space as the girls sat ramrod straight at attention. "You must protect it as such.

For here you will keep all the secrets of the sorority, secrets you can't share with anyone else, not your other friends and definitely not your parents. These traditions and history are sacred to us, passed down from our founders in 1988."

She paused and gestured to one of the framed composite portraits hanging on the living room wall. The girls in the picture stared out under teased bangs, looking smug.

"Angela will help you set up the various parts of your pledge book. You'll need a section for notes, both from our pledge meetings as well as other events you attend as a guest of a sister. As a member of OKB, if you make it that far, you'll need to be involved in the inner workings of our institution, to attend campus happenings and become a true member of the Blackthorn University community instead of merely a person who takes classes."

Courtney went on and on, detailing the pledges' responsibilities to memorize the statement of purpose and constitution of the sorority, learn facts about past members and history, schedule interviews with each sister, and collect signatures of various people across campus including their faculty advisor, officers of other fraternities and sororities, and members of certain clubs and sports teams. The pledges were also on duty for a variety of sorority events, such as the weekly Thursday night happy hours the sorority held as fundraisers. In addition, if invited as a group by any sister, they were required to attend other parties and make themselves useful by fetching drinks, offering and lighting cigarettes, and providing breath mints and gum to that sister and any of her friends.

The pledges wrote down every word in silence. No one protested or asked a clarifying question—they were intimidated by Courtney's brisk manner and clacking bootheels as she walked about the room, weaving her way in and out of the girls sitting cross-legged on the floor. Pledges weren't permitted to sit on couches.

*No nights off,* Marissa wrote. She had known about the study hall hours and thrice-weekly pledge meetings, but she had naively thought the weekend nights were their own. Now she realized they needed to make themselves available to the sisters for whatever they wanted. She glanced up to see one of her pledge sisters, Hannah, scrunching up her face at this news. Hannah had a boyfriend at home two hours away, Marissa knew. The "no nights off" rule would be hard for her.

---

BUT IT WAS ALL DOABLE, and mostly fun, as it turned out. Even with the awkward script she had to recite to the strangers she approached on the quad, such as the soccer captain and fraternity presidents, she was never alone—she always had at least one of her pledge sisters by her side.

"Hi, we're Pledge Fugitive and Pledge Klepto of Omega Kappa Beta Sorority. We are collecting signatures from important people around Blackthorn University to help us learn about the qualities of leaders on campus. Would you be so kind as to sign our pledge books?" It felt groveling and obsequious—especially with Kai since there were always follow-up quips about how the two of them sounded like a couple of criminals. There was one embarrassing occasion when they asked the wrong brother of Kappa Sig to sign as president, but most of the people they approached, even the sisters of rival sororities, offered them smiles and signed.

Marissa felt some begrudging respect. She was part of something now, just like these members of other organizations. They saw that. Even though she was only a pledge for now, she was on her way to sisterhood.

Early on, they received Big Sisters. Marissa was assigned to a sister named Phoebe, an edgy, tough senior from a wealthy Long Island family with whom she didn't have much in common, but that was okay. Big Sisters were supposed to help and guide Little Sisters during pledging, but Marissa's meetings were more functional than fun; while Kai and her Big sometimes baked cookies or watched movies together, Phoebe used the one-on-one time to help Marissa study sorority information.

And then there were the Thursday night happy hours at the OKB house. The pledges came about an hour and a half late, needing to attend study hall first, so many of the guests and sisters—the less studious ones who weren't checking on the pledges and getting their own homework done at the library—were already drunk or well on their way to it by the time Marissa and the others arrived.

The first week was fine: lighting cigarettes, handing out gum, and fetching beers whenever anyone, a sister or one of their friends, screamed "Pledge!" The pledges even got the rest of that first weekend off from attending parties with the warning that next week would be harder.

But it was different the following Thursday night at the OKB happy hour. A haze of cigarette smoke and a mass of bodies crowded the tiny kitchen onto which the back door opened. Since most of the guests were underage, the front door stayed locked and the outside light off in hopes that the backdoor business would remain undetected by police ready to dole out unspeakable fines. On a good night, the sorority might clear a few hundred dollars. It all depended on how many people had heard about the party. Anyone was welcome as long as they paid the $3 cover charge.

Marissa had been around plenty of drunk people before, not just during the freshman party scene last year but with her dad growing up. She knew the glassy look in the eyes, the slurred words that warned when someone's brain was about to go on snooze while their bodies and mouths continued moving.

So when Angela, tiny, serious Angela, of all people, the one who had been so supportive and helpful over the last couple of weeks, greeted the pledges with warm hugs and a squeakier-than-usual voice, Marissa put herself on guard.

"Pledges! Yay, you're here! Get some beer or punch! It's free for sisters and pledges since everyone else is paying to get in!" She doled out the red plastic cups, dropping a couple on the floor in the process.

Kai and the others went right over to the Rubbermaid tub full of what looked like red Kool-Aid, dipping their cups into the liquid and sipping. In a minute, Hannah had finished hers and dipped again for another.

"What's in the punch?" Marissa asked Angela, guessing college kids weren't coming to a house party and paying for Kool-Aid.

"It's grain punch! It doesn't even taste like booze! Try it!" Angela pressed her cup up to Marissa's face, grinning with red-stained teeth.

Marissa hadn't encountered grain punch at any of the parties she had attended her freshman year but knew that drinks that didn't taste like alcohol could be problematic. She also didn't like the thought of everyone dipping their used, saliva-tainted cups back in the communal receptacle.

"I think I'll get a beer instead if that's okay?"

"Pledge Fugitive!" Courtney bellowed, appearing from nowhere. "Your assistant pledge mistress kindly offered you a sip of her delightful beverage. Show your appreciation and respect to a sister. Take a sip."

Marissa complied, nodding her head and bringing the cup to her lips. It tasted fine, sweet, just like normal cherry punch, no hint of anything iniquitous. She started to hand the cup back to Angela.

Courtney shook her head, a smile on her face that didn't reach her eyes. "That simply will not do. Drink up, Pledge

Fugitive. That's an order from your pledge mistress." She gestured with her hand for Marissa to finish it.

Other sisters had squeezed their way into the kitchen. The chanting began. "Chug, chug, chug, chug!" Someone tapped out a drumroll with their fingers on the sticky kitchen counter.

She could handle this. It was just one drink; how bad could it be? No one was falling over or passed out from the stuff. She raised the beverage and let it all slide down her throat, setting the cup on the counter when finished.

Hands clapped her on the back and cheers filled the smoky air. She'd done it. Despite the feeling of unease at having chugged an unknown quantity of alcohol, she smiled.

"Not so fast." It was Danielle, the president of the sorority, wobbling a bit on towering heels, her teeth tell-tale red. "Pledges, before you start serving us, we would like you all to benefit from our wonderful hospitality. Go ahead and fill your cups. Fill them right to the brim. This is special punch, red for OKB. When we say go, you chug. The last person to finish receives a bonus cup! So, it's as if you win!"

The pledges walked toward the tub to top up. Though they'd only arrived minutes before, Marissa and Hannah had already consumed a full cup of punch. Kai caught Marissa's eye and shrugged.

Danielle leaned in, checking that everyone's cup was full.

"Ready? On your mark, get set, go!"

Marissa closed her eyes and drank as the saccharine concoction seeped out of her mouth and onto her chin. She couldn't risk a third drink. It had to be someone else, anyone else but her. Her body, unused to much alcohol, couldn't deal with another, especially when she saw how much the punch was affecting some of the sisters.

She finished and looked up. A few of her pledge sisters

were still drinking. One by one, they emptied their cups until it was just Hannah.

"I guess I win?" Hannah asked, setting down her cup.

Angela grabbed and refilled it. "Here's your prize!" Hannah accepted and drank, faster this time, the red liquid spilling out from the corners of her mouth, carving rivulets through her thick foundation and forming a long red stain on her white shirt. In the ten or so minutes since she had entered the house, she had consumed three full drinks.

The pledges inched their way through the kitchen, past the living room where some people were trying to bounce quarters into shot glasses on the coffee table, down to the basement so they could begin their duties.

Until about twenty minutes before, Marissa had been finishing up her homework in the quiet comfort of the library. Now, she was in a different world, the flip side of college. She probably wasn't drunk yet, even with how fast she drank, but she still clutched onto the handrail as she descended the rickety stairs into the maw of the party, where the suffocating heat from sweaty bodies reached up at them while D.J. Kool's "Let Me Clear My Throat" blared from a boom box.

The party atmosphere—the music, crowd, and nonstop smoke—added to the tipsy feeling Marissa was already experiencing. She wanted to go home and lie down, drink some water to slow down the alcohol's effect, and be alert for her class the next morning. But she was a pledge, and her job was to help run the party.

Saying "Excuse me," she moved her way through the guests toward the keg, cognizant of other people's sweat and body parts touching her.

A few of the sisters clocked the pledges as they progressed closer, a line led by Jessica. One of the girls they hadn't seen much of except at parties, Amanda, raised her voice. "Finally, the plebes are here! We've been waiting for y'all to take over!"

She held out the nozzle of the beer tap with one hand and her empty cup with the other. "Fill me up! No foam!"

Jessica obliged while another sister, Tara, stepped forward. "Don't forget about your responsibilities. There are five of you, so you can divide and conquer. Two of you go back upstairs and take care of things there. Three of you will stay down here. And who's in charge of fundraising?"

Kai shot up her hand. "I am! I have the bottle of Bailey's here." She indicated her backpack.

Tara continued. "Shots are a dollar a pop. You guys keep the money for pledging expenses like the cigarettes, gum, and breakfasts you need to buy."

They'd already learned that Saturday mornings were for sister breakfasts: Amongst the group of them, they had to purchase, prepare, and deliver a brown bag to each sister's residence containing items like a fresh bagel, packet of cream cheese, and bottle of OJ.

"And don't forget: You *need* this cash, so even sisters have to pay for their shots, no matter what anyone tries to tell you." Tara delegated roles to all five pledges, and Marissa felt grateful that someone was still acting responsibly and looking out for them. It made her feel like there was a purpose for pledging, not that they were merely at the beck and call of plastered sisters wanting to be served and entertained.

By eleven, most of the partygoers had left, off to other parties, the bar (if they were twenty-one or had good fake IDs), or maybe even home to bed to sleep it off and wake up for their classes Friday morning. The pledges began the task of cleaning up: throwing away the plastic cups littering the basement and upstairs, wiping the counters, and mopping up the floors. With five of them working together, they could be done within the hour, and then they could finally leave.

Marissa had pretty much sobered up. Even though she had drunk a beer at the request of a sister, not having to chug it this time, at least, but to "lighten up and enjoy herself," she'd also sneaked off to the kitchen to drink a few cups of tap water.

Hannah wasn't looking too good. After those three grain punches, she'd ended up doing a shot of Bailey's that a sister bought her, and Marissa saw her drinking a beer later, some of which had spilled on her shirt to accompany the red stain, and that's just what she *witnessed* Hannah consume. Jessica had brought her water earlier and urged her to drink it, but Hannah had swatted her away. Now, though a pledge sister had handed her a paper towel, Hannah was pretty much slumped against the kitchen counter, not cleaning or even standing up.

Angela had kept drinking, as well. She barked out commands once in a while, reminders to clean the bathroom or whatnot, but her words were so slurred that the pledges couldn't always tell what she meant. Eventually, she crashed onto the couch and started snoring.

Tara had long since left, muttering that she had an exam the next morning. And with Angela passed out, no one was there to stop the hazing when, past midnight, five sisters came home from the bar.

# CHAPTER 15

Dark clouds hung in the air the day of Hadley's funeral, low and gray, sucking out what little life force we mourners had to offer. A chill bit through my thin jacket, worsened by the wind that swirled my hair around my head as I hurried into the funeral home.

Hadley's parents had emailed me with the pertinent information, a formal invitation after their oral request. I didn't have classes on Tuesday mornings, so I didn't even have to call off work.

The Parkers greeted me with warm hugs like I was a family member instead of their dead daughter's professor. Even though I was known to stiffen when embraced, I squeezed them back, trying to convey my sorrow and care with touch.

Mrs. Parker looked worse than before, her eyes red and puffy, her face drawn and lined. Since the last time I had seen her, just a few days ago, she seemed even more shrunken, as if she was folding in on herself, diminished from grief.

"We're so thankful that you came. It means so much to know that our girl had a professor who cared about her," she

"Of course." I knew these words weren't enough, but I could hardly say that I was glad to be here. None of us were. On a Tuesday morning, Hadley should be sitting in class, not laid out in a coffin.

Another mourner came to greet the Parkers, so I took my cue to excuse myself. As custom demanded, I walked toward the coffin to say goodbye.

It was a closed casket. Whatever the Parkers' wishes may have been, far too much time had passed for the alternative. Not only was Hadley's body discovered long after her death, but the police had needed to perform the autopsy, delaying proceedings even more. I was relieved that I didn't have to look at her; I knew that people often wanted one last look at the deceased, but I found the idea of pumping a body full of embalming fluid, rouging the pale cheeks, and stitching nostrils and lips shut unnerving.

After the hospital released Emma's body, we had her taken to a crematorium, not going through a funeral home with its heartbreaking tiny coffins specially designed for babies. I didn't want a funeral—I couldn't handle the well-meaning but hurtful comments that would have come from David's family and our colleagues. "It was God's plan" provided me zero consolation that the baby for whom I'd imagined a full existence had never breathed air into her lungs, hadn't lived outside my body. David had begged me for it, saying that she should be buried in his family plot, but I held my ground. I didn't want to imagine her delicate flesh decaying off her bones, and I couldn't bear for her remains to reside all the way in Connecticut. Yes, Emma was a Hanlon, but she was also *mine*.

But today it was the Parkers' heartbreak rather than my own. Though I thought of my little girl and the person she might have become every single day, at least time had dulled my despair.

I stood in front of the coffin, an ornate white affair covered in pink and red roses, and thought of the girl inside of it. All that hope, all that potential, cast aside, and for what? Her body would be "laid to rest" today, but would her parents ever properly rest again while their daughter's killer went free?

Looking at the Parkers in the front row of chairs as the minister gave his speech, all I saw was their sadness. Based on their mannerisms—their bowed heads and hunched shoulders —they seemed to be ensconced in the grief stage. Anger at the world and the person who did this to their daughter would come later.

It was a small gathering attended by mostly middle-aged and elderly mourners with a few young people thrown in. The service hadn't been listed in the paper; I had looked. The Parkers were probably concerned that true crime enthusiasts and looky-loos might crash, anxious for podcast and Instagram fodder.

I didn't recognize any students from Blackthorn, but President Lattimore was there, standoffish but distinguished in a well-cut suit. I couldn't shake the feeling that this was a PR maneuver. I doubted that he showed up for the funerals of every single student who died, but Hadley's death was newsworthy. I watched as he greeted the Parkers but then took a seat and fiddled with his phone before the service began. Maybe he was crafting his next email to prove how caring he was. He didn't make eye contact or greet me, and I decided not to make a move.

One more familiar face from the town of Blackthorn stuck out from the crowd: Detective Jake Ruiz. Wearing funeral black in a suit that probably cost about a tenth of the one Lattimore wore, he still looked at least ten times better. He sat in the back, no sign of his partner. When he saw me staring, he responded with a somber wave.

About fifteen minutes after I arrived, speakers in the walls began playing soft classical music, and the Parkers took their seats in the front row of chairs. A short, round man walked up to the lectern.

"Good morning. My name is Keith Riemann, director of Riemann Funeral Home. We are here today to honor the life of Hadley Vanessa Parker, who has been called home to God." He went on from there with a brief tribute to Hadley: who she was, what she was like as a child, her interests, etc. He said nothing about the manner of her death. There was no need, as everyone in the room had likely watched the press conference and learned the gruesome details.

As he finished his speech, Riemann said, "I will now introduce Hadley's favorite college professor, Ms. Marissa Owen, who will read a poem for us."

I walked up to the stand and resisted the urge to correct my title and name—this was Hadley's day. Fulfilling the request of the Parkers, I read "Annabel Lee."

I'd done innumerable readings and conference presentations, usually for far larger audiences, but with Hadley's parents and other relatives waiting for me to speak, I noticed the tremor in my hands as I unfolded my printout. While I had memorized the poem "many and many a year ago" and practiced the recitation as recently as that morning, I felt a great rush of anguish.

Poor Annabel Lee, the innocent girl who lived to love but perished away. Poe was known for writing about beautiful women who died before their time and were missed by a narrator, often an obsessive one.

But here, at Hadley's funeral, I thought about how real life's bleakness outshone that of fiction by the dark master. Annabel Lee, Lenore, Eleanora, Ligeia, heck, even Poe's mother, foster mother, and wife, died tragically, yet they all succumbed to illness, not murder. Poe once wrote, "The death of a beautiful woman is, unquestionably, the most poetical topic in the world."

I could appreciate that in fiction, but not in reality. Hadley's death held no poetry—all I saw was tragedy.

I didn't know what comfort Hadley's parents would find even if the full circumstances of her death were brought to light. Would it bring them peace to put a name and face on the demon who took their only child away?

Fighting my anxiety, I began the reading, and my voice manifested as clear rather than shaky. I looked out at the audience, meeting the sorrowful but appreciative gaze of the Parkers, the attentive look of consternation on Ruiz's face, and the stony stare of President Lattimore, whom I imagined to be thinking about the other tasks of his day.

Poe's haunting words continued to spill forth from my mouth as I scanned the faces of the men in the crowd from young to old, wondering, *Was it you?* I knew that killers sometimes attended the funerals of their victims. Not that I knew for certain that there *was* a killer. Hadley's death was suspicious, and crimes had definitely occurred since her body was cleaned up and moved from the scene, but no one but the person who did it knew if her death was accidental or intentional.

I considered saying a few words of my own about Hadley when I finished the reading, but I didn't want to overstep, and no one else had offered condolences. It didn't seem to be that type of funeral. Following a murmured, "Thank you," I walked back to my seat.

---

AFTERWARD, there was some milling about from the attendees. Lattimore took off right away after a perfunctory exchange with the Parkers. Perhaps I was being too hard on him—he had made an appearance, after all, and most likely had a much fuller and more important schedule than I did. My own afternoon consisted of driving back home, teaching my class, and grading papers. Also, in practical matters, as president, he needed to worry about the university's sustainability. As an instructor at Blackthorn, even a temporary one, my livelihood depended on the university making it through this.

If enrollment suffered, if parents pulled their students out of school in fear that what happened to Hadley might occur again, my guess was that the university would prevail. With a population of ten thousand counting the graduate students, enough students would remain so that BU wouldn't go under. Probably.

Mr. and Mrs. Parker only had the one child. The university would heal, but would *they*? Someday, years from now, Hadley's death would be a blip on Blackthorn's history. But to her family, Hadley's absence would hang like a shroud over their happiness for the rest of their lives.

The Parkers caught me staring at them and came over, their forced smiles tight on their faces. "We'll never forget you for being here with us today." Mrs. Parker placed a cold, chapped hand on the bare skin of my forearm. The poor woman did not seem well.

"I'll never forget you, either." It was true. We were linked together as childless parents, even if not in the same way. I'd also never forget Hadley. It always shocked me how a student could sit in my class all semester, even a strong student, and disappear from my memory within a year while others lingered. I've forgotten an entire person but remembered small details about what another student wrote in a paper or brought up in class discussion. I liked to think I would have remembered Hadley for years to come due to her passion and intelligence, not just for her awful demise.

"If only she had come to us, whatever she chose to do about the baby, we would have supported her," Hadley's father said. "To think that she didn't even talk to us about it hurts the most, that maybe *she* decided to go through with it. We didn't even know she had a boyfriend."

I didn't share what I knew of college hookup culture; Hadley's pregnancy wasn't evidence of an actual relationship.

"None of this means that Hadley loved you less," I said. "And the police will get to the bottom of what happened."

I made my way out of the funeral home with one last look at Hadley's coffin, which would soon be buried in a local cemetery. Despite all that potential, she would never go on to live a full life where she could achieve her dreams. Instead, her body would be left to rot underground.

I needed to flee this house of death and go back outdoors where there was hope. I closed my eyes for a moment to shut out the sadness.

That's when I felt a tap on my shoulder.

## Chapter 16

"Hi. I was wondering if we could speak a bit."

By now, I knew that voice, the low rumble that could be a commanding boom if he wanted. But Jake Ruiz was too polite for that. He understood that this, a place of mourning, was a setting for respect, not force.

"Sure." I looked around, noticing the thinning crowd and lack of places to go other than this main room. "Should we go outside?"

"It's pretty windy out. Can we get coffee? I know a diner nearby." He lowered his volume further so that I needed to lean in to hear. "I'd like to share some new information about the case."

I nodded, trying to extinguish the embarrassed flush that had risen to my cheeks at his close proximity. "Yes. Okay."

If he noticed, he didn't let on. "It's about a five-minute walk or a one-minute drive. Whatever you prefer, but parking in town is a pain in the ass. My niece is a student at the college, and we've gone there when I've visited."

*His niece.* I hadn't thought about Jake *that* much since I'd met him, not even after the initial brusqueness passed. Now I was imagining his family and caught myself before taking a peek at his ring finger.

Then I *did* peek. Nothing there, but I knew that lots of married men didn't wear wedding rings.

*Get a hold of yourself. This is about Hadley.*

"It's a mom-and-pop place, just a crappy little diner. But it has a certain charm to it, and the coffee's good. And you like coffee, right? I remember you drinking it that time I came to your apartment." A smile rose to his lips before he suppressed it and went back into serious mode.

I glanced at the Parkers, who were huddled together near the coffin, and gave them a final nod, even though they weren't looking. I would probably never see them again in person, but I might catch them on the news if Hadley's case was ever solved. Since Jake was obviously working hard, driving down to York just to attend the funeral, maybe that would happen.

"Let's walk," I said. I hadn't been in York much, but my time in Baltimore made me yearn to avoid city parking whenever possible, and I didn't want the awkwardness of deciding if we should drive together.

We opened the heavy door and discovered that the clouds had lifted and the sun was shining. Though the wind ravaged my hair and nipped at my face, I couldn't help but feel a lightness as I left death behind me.

---

WITH DOWNTOWN YORK's honking cars and the wind's whooshing, there was little time for small talk before reaching our destination. We stepped into the diner.

"There's a Starbucks nearby, but you don't strike me as that kind of person. I figured you'd appreciate a good old-fashioned diner," he said as we sat at an unadorned booth with a cracked laminate table.

"You've misjudged me," I said, smiling. "You must not have noticed my crazy collection of Starbucks mugs at the apartment. I buy them wherever I travel, and I'm a sucker for a venti skinny vanilla latte. But I like diners, too."

It felt easy, talking to him about nothing important, especially after the heavy morning and whatever he wanted to share with me. Maybe this banter was *too* lighthearted for the circumstances.

A waitress ambled over to take our order, the jowls of her fleshy face lifting in a grin when she saw him. "Jake! You're back! But where's your niece? I've never seen you without her."

"Unfortunately, Cheryl, I'm here on police business today, but I may get a chance to stop by her dorm and say hi if she's free."

So he'd been here so often that he knew the waitresses by name, showing he was more involved than the average uncle.

I admired when people were close to their families, envied it really. It had been almost a year since I'd spoken to my sister, and our last conversation was fraught with tension. We'd texted a few times after that, but not often, and I hadn't seen my nephews, four and six by now, since the little one was in diapers. We'd been so close as children, but after I left for college and Mom died of lung cancer, I'd barely been back home. Annie hadn't fully forgiven me for leaving her and Dad. As for Dad, he never reached out, but I called once a month, always on a Sunday afternoon before he got too loaded.

Cheryl returned with the coffee pot and two mugs. As I lifted mine to my lips, ready for the caffeine boost to which I was addicted, Jake busied himself adding several creamers and a long pour of sugar.

"Hey, I have a tough job. I'll take some comfort in my life. Stop judging."

Part of me longed to pretend this was a date, that we were two adults getting to know each other. He had been so reserved in most of our interactions that it delighted me to notice the crinkles around his eyes when he smiled. Even his slightly crooked eye tooth added to the appeal, a deviation in the perfection. Still, we were here on business.

"So. You said you had an update for me?"

Jake's expression changed immediately, back in detective mode. "Yes. I thought you should know this since you were the one who brought it to my attention. I've learned some information about those Greek letters you noticed. Based on what I found out, Psi Omega Phi Phi seems to be a real thing, and it *is* a secret sorority."

"Really?" I was surprised that, in the age of the internet and social media, I hadn't been able to unearth anything myself during some insomnia-driven searches I'd done since discovering Hadley's scribble on the peer review paper.

"College students are the *worst* at keeping their mouths shut. Half the drama I hear from students is because one supposed friend told someone else's business."

Some college students *could* keep secrets, keep them for decades, in fact, but those stakes were higher, and I wasn't about to share *that*.

"I talked to that Director of Greek Life, Rob Healy, and it was a pretty dead end. He said there was no reason for a sorority to form underground, that Greek life is accepted and even supported on campus. He told me how it's regulated in response to hazing events across the country and even at Blackthorn. He acted really proud of how the university has eliminated hazing. He even handed me this." Jake reached inside his pocket and produced a creased pamphlet with garish red lettering: Stop Hazing Now.

I took a cursory glance. In theory, the strategies could work, but reality was a different story. I sighed. "Jake, I don't know what you know about Greek life in general, but it's unrealistic that hazing has been eradicated. Having a mandatory faculty advisor and being required to participate in campus events and community service doesn't mean that any campus employee is overseeing what happens in the basement of a frat house. Even the national organizations with their own rules on *top* of the university's rules can't exert complete control over an individual chapter."

"You don't buy it? You don't think he was straight with me?"

"I don't think he was *lying*. It's what the university chooses to believe, a convenient fiction—the clean-cut leaders of the organizations show up to meetings in ties and dresses, and they shake hands with university officials like responsible young adults, and everyone pretends everything's fine. The truth is that most pledges won't report hazing; even if they end up quitting, the social pressure of tattling is far too great."

"What makes you so sure? Are students telling you what happens in those frat house basements? And have you reported it? You're a mandatory reporter, aren't you?"

I rolled my eyes in frustration. "No, they're not *telling* me about hazing, but I *know*. I was a part of Greek life, too. Some things don't change, and that's not just at Blackthorn. Years ago, at Sainsbury, one of my advisees told me she was transferring because she wanted to get away after quitting pledging. She said she felt iced out of everything, that the girls in the sorority stopped talking to her, even her pledge sisters to whom she'd become so close. And even beyond that, friends from other Greek organizations turned their backs on her. I asked her if she wanted to report anything to the Dean of Students, and she asked me, 'What would I even say? That people don't want to be friends with me?' She didn't speak a word about how she was treated while pledging—if she was hazed or not—but the aftermath was bad enough that she left the university." I took a sip of my coffee and gave him a moment to digest.

"I've heard about some big college hazing cases, of course, but I've never been called in as an officer. I mean, hell, we have our own sort of hazing in the police force—'rookie initiation.' It's supposed to be a rite of passage, you know, an 'enter the brotherhood' type of thing, but I've seen it get out of hand. Do you think all Greek organizations haze their pledges?"

"I think it depends on how you define hazing. Don't all organizations, not just Greek ones, require prospective members to prove themselves? You should've seen what I went through to become tenured and promoted at my previous university. Obviously, it's different than pledging but similar in that you're on probation, and seasoned people will judge you and have expectations of you until you cross a threshold. I don't know what made my advisee quit—she didn't say. But something changed her mind about becoming a member, whether or not it was because she was mistreated. Then again, I quit the musical in high school, and it wasn't because I was hazed. I wasn't enjoying it and didn't really connect with the other students who were in it. I joined because my friend did, and then we weren't friends anymore, and I wanted out. I didn't want to waste my time doing something I didn't want anymore."

Jake's eyebrows raised in question for a moment, like he wanted to know more, but my personal friendship history wasn't the point of this discussion. "So, Marissa, why do you think this Psi Omega Phi Phi would want to be secret if fraternities and sororities are kind of doing whatever they want anyway?"

"I don't know. I think it's easy to get away with stuff. When I was a freshman in college, one of the bigger frats got in serious trouble after some freshmen—not pledges, just random freshmen who had paid to party there—were taken to the ER for alcohol poisoning. The frat was put under the microscope by the university."

I wasn't there that night, but I could still remember the drama that followed, with the boys' parents threatening to sue. It had been messy, but nothing really changed after that.

"Campus cops would drive by the frat house every night to check that they weren't having parties, and the guys were threatened with fines and expulsion. But they didn't lose their charter after all that," I explained. "They just kept a lower profile and still got to have pledges after one probationary semester."

I allowed Cheryl to top off my lukewarm coffee. As much as I wanted that jolt of energy, the charged conversation had caused me to neglect it. I felt her eyeing me under those penciled-on brows and horn-rimmed glasses. At least in her mid-sixties, she exuded more concern than jealousy that Jake was with a woman in her diner. She buzzed around us like a fly, adding what seemed like drops at a time to Jake's coffee. A graveyard of empty creamer containers lay around his mug.

I took a sip and gave it some more consideration. "I think it's *weird* that there's an underground sorority when there's already a thick air of secrecy around Greek organizations. The traditions, mottos, everything, really, are supposed to be known only by the members. But *you* told *me* that you found something out about them. I've been going on and on about Greek life in general but don't have a clue about this organization or what it has to do, if anything, with Hadley's death, or even what she was up to before she died. Who are they? What did you find?"

Jake's eyes lit up as he prepared for the big reveal. "You said you were searching for the name, right? But they're secret —that seems to be their whole deal. Even if they use the Greek letters, they distance themselves from the rest of the Greek organizations. No one's supposed to know about them. So I started thinking about what Greeks call themselves. Some use the Roman alphabet equivalent. Alpha Sigma Tau calls themselves AST, for example. And some go by abbreviations of at least some of their Greek letters, like Sigma Phi Epsilon goes by Sig Ep. But when I was talking to Healy, he referred to an organization as the Crows, and I thought that sounded unusual since it didn't sound like Greek letters. I asked, and he said they were known as that but that their full name was Alpha Chi Rho. Chi plus rho equals Crow, sort of.

"So then I started brainstorming. My mom was always doing those Jumbles when I was growing up, you know? Where you figure out the word that's mixed up? An anagram? I'd help her sometimes, plus those cryptograms where one letter gets substituted for another." Jake grabbed that tiny notebook out of his pocket and scribbled the Greek letters and then their Roman correspondents, holding it for me to see. "Psi Omega Phi Phi. POPP, sort of. So I searched the internet, even the campus newspapers, for that instead of the letters. And after an annoying search of nothing, I finally found the Poppies."

I stared at him, a cat-that-ate-the-canary expression on his face, and pictured him hunched over his desk like Legrand in Poe's story "The Goldbug," figuring out the cipher. He was pleased for getting closer to the truth by cracking the code, but this new development didn't prove any real answers.

"*What* did you uncover about them? And how do we know that Hadley was pledging if you didn't find any clues other than those Greek letters I showed you on the paper?"

"From what I understand, they stay small, no more than twenty members at a time, which is part of how they keep everything secret. Twenty girls out of ten thousand students won't raise suspicions as long as they're careful. And it looks like they've *been* careful. Did you ever read the Greek life gossip page of the student paper at Blackthorn?"

"Yes. It's horrible. Obscene at times, even. There's all kinds of dirt that the organizations print about themselves and each other, thinly veiled innuendo and even petty crimes. If any university official took a close look at those blurbs, students would be in trouble for sure."

Jake nodded after taking a quick slurp of his coffee. "I don't even want to think about what some of those references meant, especially since my niece is a college student. But here's the thing: All sorts of organizations have provided their own write-ups and been mentioned in others, but the Poppies weren't mentioned once, in any capacity, out of all the years of issues I scanned."

I started becoming irritated at how he was parsing out the details. Even though I appreciated being kept in the loop, his comments were rather long and rambling. "Where *did* you find information about them, then?"

"Facebook. Police find out tons of information about people and cases from there as well as other social media platforms. About five years ago, a student posted a number of references to the Poppies. The posts were deleted within hours, either by her or someone else, but I was able to recover them with some help from my buddy who's a digital forensics tech. And one of the many secrets—nothing damning but maybe interesting—she shared was that the Poppies' pledges attach a flower patch to their backpacks. When we searched Hadley's room after her body was discovered, we found this."

Jake unlocked his iPhone, scrolled through some pictures, and showed me a photo that made my heart lurch: Hadley's tie-dyed backpack, the very one she had packed to the brim and hauled to my classroom and office in the early weeks of the semester, with a tiny red poppy affixed to the pocket.

"Okay, that's pretty much proof she was pledging with

what that girl wrote on Facebook, but is there any reason to think this group was up to anything atrocious compared to normal Greek life shenanigans? Is this just run-of-the-mill sorority secrecy with the extra 'underground' aspect thrown in for a bonus?"

Despite the evidence he'd dug up, I wasn't convinced that Jake understood the depth of Greek life clandestinity; even something innocuous, like spilling the beans to a nonmember about how to do a special handshake, could land a pledge, or even a fully-initiated brother or sister, in hot water with the rest of the group.

"I'm not sure. The girl was clearly upset. She wrote six posts in about twenty minutes." He flipped back a few pages in his notebook. "There was some angry but vague stuff like, 'The Poppies think they own this university,' and 'Don't trust anyone, even your sister.' And there were some mild secrets about the poppy patch and a necklace, but then it got weird, like 'Horseshoes are supposed to be lucky but my luck changed when I met the Poppies, and now I can't get my life back.'"

I pictured Hadley back in my office the day she asked me whether or not she should join a sorority. "What did it say about the necklace?"

He scanned through his phone and read to me. "'They sneak in your room and give you a fancy necklace with an invitation to join them in a secret location two days later and tell you to destroy the note. If you show up but say no to pledging, or if you don't comply with the rules as a pledge, they rip it off your neck.' That's kind of screwed up, not to mention breaking and entering, but it sounds like another of these silly traditions."

I shook my head. "I don't know. It could be important. Hadley had a horseshoe necklace. I remember her fidgeting with it, so that's more confirmation that she was pledging the

Poppies—that they had invited her by then, and I guess she was still thinking about it. But back to this Facebook girl. She was upset, but what happened after that?"

Jake took in a deep breath. "That's where it gets particularly compelling. According to records, she withdrew from Blackthorn the next day after posting. No one had reacted or commented before she deleted her posts, but someone may have seen them. Then she checked herself into a psychiatric ward, where she stayed for three weeks.

"She left the facility and was given the keys to her car, according to the hospital, and her credit card was used at a Wawa and a Walmart in the next couple days. But there's no sign of her after that. Her car was found smashed in a ditch a week after the last credit card record. No trace of her or of her blood—just some bags of her possessions, but no one could tell if anything was missing, if she could've walked away after getting in the wreck.

"There was no report of a car accident with another car, but she crashed into *some*thing and she had to go *some*where. And she hadn't used her cell phone or logged into social media since before she checked herself in for treatment, and there was never a missing person's report filed. The only record in the system is because the plates matched her name on that abandoned car."

"This happened five years ago and she never resurfaced? And her family's not hiding her out somewhere?"

"No sign of her. She didn't really *have* family. She was a foster kid who wasn't ever adopted. Her biological parents are dead, and she bounced around from house to house as a kid, never really connecting with the foster parents. Not a bad kid, according to the one foster mom I spoke with over the phone, but quiet, aloof. She was on scholarship at Blackthorn. She's exactly the kind of girl who could disappear without anyone making a fuss."

No family. A loner. On scholarship.

In some ways, this girl sounded like Hadley, but Hadley had loving parents. In more ways, she sounded like *me* as a college student. This girl disappeared and no one knew what happened to her. No one really cared.

I massaged my temples and hoped it wasn't what it seemed. "She could be in hiding and safe and sound, don't you think? Maybe she started over under a new name. Maybe she was worried that she'd be in trouble with the Poppies and managed to get a fake ID or something. And if she had mental health issues, it's possible she was overly paranoid about things."

"Marissa, I've been a detective for almost twenty years now, and I was a beat cop before that. I've seen some horrible shit. The chance that a nineteen-year-old girl with hardly any resources—less than a hundred dollars in her bank account— who just checked out of a mental health facility, for God's sake, the chance that she's safe and sound is slim to none. The fact that both she and Hadley are linked to the Poppies gives me a strong sense that they are one dangerous group of girls. How they contributed to Hadley's death, if they did at all, I don't know, but I'm gonna find out."

After this pronouncement, his face stern and flinty, he signaled for Cheryl to bring the check.

"What happens now?" My voice came out as barely a whisper.

"What happens *now* is that I need to stop by to try and check in on my niece and then drive back to Blackthorn and get back to work. I have Welch combing through Hadley's belongings, both the ones recovered from her body and the ones in her room, to find any shred of evidence that could implicate the Poppies, anything that might show their involvement or give a hint to the girls' identities."

Jake had been almost cheerful when telling me about his

discovery of the Poppies, but his manner had grown darker and more closed off as he recounted the questionable fate of this mysterious girl. This *nameless* girl.

"Jake, just one more thing. Who *was* this girl? It's such a horrible story, that she had mental health issues and no family, and that no one even noticed she was missing. What was her name, if you can tell me?"

He closed his eyes and nodded. "Sure. I've told you this much already. I thought you should know since you helped lead me to this. Her name was Audrey Quarto."

*Audrey Quarto.* Missed by none, allowed to disappear into history as if she never existed.

He paid the bill, waving away the dollars I held out, and we left the diner to go our separate ways, the easy comradery having faded. The clouds were back, the sky gloomy once more.

# CHAPTER 17
## THEN

The sisters who showed up at the sorority house were all drunk—and belligerent. Charity was yammering on about how they got kicked out of the bar because she'd hooked up with the boyfriend of some girl who worked there, something about her ID even though it was a really good fake—no, it wasn't fake, but the girl in the license kind of looked like her, and she had practiced earlier so she could recite Lisette Shaeffer's birthdate and address in case the bouncer quizzed her.

Like Marissa, Kai had monitored her alcohol intake that night. The two shared a nervous glance as the sisters came barreling in, dropping light jackets and heels like a snake sheds its skin, stumbling through the doorway and disrupting the calm of the pledges' cleaning routine, breaking the promise that they'd get to leave.

Phoebe, her delicate features screwed up like she was sucking a lemon, was pissed off, and mainly at Charity—she kept sniping at her, growling under her breath. But when her eyes fell upon the five pledges, most of whom appeared at least somewhat alert with mops or garbage bags in hand, she smirked, and Marissa knew then that she was willing to transfer her anger to them.

"Why are all of you still cleaning? Shouldn't you be done by now? You think you can just stay in our house and waste our electricity?" Her Long Island accent more pronounced than usual, Phoebe was heavily intoxicated.

A quick glance at Angela—the one who often gently advocated for the pledges when sisters acted unreasonably—confirmed that no one would save them from Phoebe's wrath. Angela was still snoring away on the couch, drunk.

Jessica was the one who answered. "We're sorry, Sisters. We're just finishing up and leaving." The pledges had been schooled to speak with deference to the sisters even when criticized for following orders. *A sister is never wrong.* Jessica moved to return the broom to the cupboard. Everything was pristine, anyway, and it was late.

"And what the fuck is wrong with Pledge Gonzo?" Charity asked. Hannah, whose pledge name was earned for her love of Hunter S. Thompson, Marissa hoped, rather than her larger-than-average nose, had slumped to the floor, mouth open and drooling.

"I think she might have had too much to drink and needs to go to sleep." Marissa surprised herself by speaking up and retreated, overcompensating. "We are sorry for her indiscretions."

"And look who showed up!" Abby this time, a loud redhead who played lacrosse. The pledges were required to go to the home games as a show of support, so they knew how tough she could be both on and off the field despite her diminutive size and prominent lisp. "Pledge Fugitive, how kind of you to attend our humble gathering!"

All this even though Marissa had only missed that first sorority function for work. "I'm sorry. I won't miss anything again." She looked down at the floor. Angela had drilled into their heads that pledges should be subservient and passive.

"That's right, or else," Danielle spat out at them.

*Who was the real Danielle?* Marissa wondered. *The friendly girl they met at rush, the introvert who didn't acknowledge them, or this new, bitter version who forced them to drink and was now threatening them?*

Danielle's next words clarified it all. "Pledges, we're heading to the basement. Time for a *real* function."

They had no choice but to follow.

---

MARISSA'S THIGHS BURNED. Since pledging had started, she hadn't made it to the gym even once. Yet here she was, at almost one a.m. on a Friday morning when she had class in a few hours, doing wall squats.

"Don't you give up! Girls, keep your asses on that wall!" More authoritarian than motivational workout coach, Phoebe screeched her demands, beer in her hand precariously close to its tipping point.

Hannah was incoherent. Her pledge sisters had practically carried her downstairs, and the sisters hadn't argued when she failed to comply with their orders. Passed out in the corner, Hannah had wet herself, her urine pooling on the concrete floor.

"Gross," Charity said. "That girl has problems."

Marissa's anxiety dwindled when she heard Hannah emit a massive snore. Hannah was fine. Marissa needed to focus—that 90-degree angle was impossible to maintain.

"Some of you girls don't seem like you can handle this," Abby said, each *s* catching more than usual since she was drinking. "That's okay, I guess. We're not about to circle your fat or anything, so don't worry." She laughed, harsh and guttural. "But if you can't hack the physical side, you sure as fuck better know the brain side. Plebes, what is the mission of Omega Kappa Beta?"

"Omega Kappa Beta's mission is to forge bonds of sisterhood while enhancing personal excellence and achievement." The pledges, minus Hannah, spoke almost in unison, though Janelle lagged a bit—she struggled with performance. They had all said this so many times, had practiced it together and on their own, that it felt as ingrained inside of them as the Pledge of Allegiance.

The sisters went on and on, quizzing them about current and past sisters as well as sorority history. Despite the late hour and inebriation, the girls were doing well. Too well.

"Do we still have beer? You pledges seem way too sober. I feel like you're not even having fun." Phoebe glowered at the pledges in the dim light of the single naked bulb. "I'm so sorry. Are we not fun?" She puckered her lips into an exaggerated pout.

Kai answered this time, her words over the top. "We are so grateful to be included in your fun evening!"

"Thank you for your enthusiasm, Pledge Klepto!" Phoebe's sarcastic words penetrated the space. "Last I knew, before the fucking bar with that fucking bitch, we hadn't kicked our keg. Why don't you be a sweetie and get us all a beer. Now. Girls, you are *still* included in our 'fun evening.'"

Phoebe yawned, her mouth opening wide, and sucked in air with a snort. "Get me a beer. I want one more beer. You plebes don't even know how nice we're being to you. I have philosophy class at ten tomorrow, yet here I am hanging out with all of you. *That* is some dedication."

As Phoebe spoke, Kai filled the plastic cups stacked next to the bar and handed them out, first to sisters and then pledges.

Marissa accepted her cup. She had to. She kicked it back, and, when Charity brought out the vodka, she took the shot.

When Phoebe demanded another chugging contest, she complied. She didn't want to disappoint her Big Sister.

*This* is what you had to do to be a sister. They'd all been through it before, and they had to pass it on.

When she finally woke up the next morning, at eleven a.m., somehow in her own dorm room, in her own bed, Marissa couldn't remember how she'd gotten home. But she'd sure as hell slept through her class. Running to the bathroom, a nauseated feeling in her gut, she wondered why, again, she was part of it all.

But she'd come this far and didn't want to stop. If she backed out now, she'd lose everything, all these weeks of servitude with nothing to show for it. Maybe she'd even lose Kai. No—she was in it until the end. Nothing, no matter what the sisters pulled next, would make her quit.

# Chapter 18

I brooded over it all for the next couple of days, trying to distract myself by focusing on my job. By Friday night, with no plans per usual, I hadn't heard anything more from Jake about the case and told myself that it wasn't my business, that I had to move on. As much as I tried to concentrate on the essays from my freshmen comp classes, I couldn't get my head around them. Part of me didn't care, not with more important thoughts stalking my consciousness.

*Audrey Quarto. The Poppies.* I couldn't shake these words, not after everything Jake had said in the diner. They felt engraved in my brain.

It's hard to keep a stride going when grading, so my method was to get through at least two or three depending on the assignment before allowing myself a short break, but I couldn't help it—I was stopping after each one, even though I knew that my future self would pay for my lack of progress in the next couple of days.

I gave in to temptation and focused on my obsession, checking Facebook and Instagram but finding nothing. Jake said Audrey's Facebook posts about the Poppies had been deleted, but I was hoping to come across her old posts. Her account appeared deactivated—there was no one by that name, and I didn't know her middle name to see if she was listed under something else. Did I really expect to find out more than the cops had, especially Jake, who had already ascertained so much? Of course not, but I wanted more of an idea of who Audrey was and what she had in common with Hadley.

With *me*.

Not that *I* had been in the Poppies, but my stomach roiled in queasiness at the parallelism of our backgrounds. If I had gone missing in college, would anyone have looked for *me*? Like Audrey, I didn't have much of a family, either.

Hadley's and Audrey's cases, if Audrey even *had* a case, since she was not officially a missing person and was maybe just living off the grid somewhere, weren't very similar on the surface. Hadley was found mutilated and dead, while Audrey checked herself into a mental health treatment center and later disappeared.

Two different girls associated with the Poppies, five years apart, and at least one tragic outcome.

An organization that wasn't recognized by the institution and that was based on secrets couldn't be innocent, could it? Might this all be a terrible coincidence, with the Poppies' extra layer of secrecy as inane as any other covert sorority ritual? I thought back to my own sorority days, how we weren't even allowed to share our sorority constitution, as if anyone were possibly interested in *that*.

Walking away from my computer, I went through non-thinking rituals like changing my bedsheets, feeding Norman, and throwing together a taco salad for dinner, my mind searching for answers.

I googled the Poppies and didn't uncover anything relevant after sifting through references to the actual flower, a sixties band, and a nineties duo. I listened to a few songs on YouTube and looked up lyrics, trying to find meaning, but all I discovered was that I preferred the earlier music.

Jake had told me that there was almost nothing on Audrey on the internet, but I had to see for myself. If I googled myself, which I didn't like to do, I could easily find over a hundred thousand results, most of which were professionally-oriented: mentions of articles and essays I'd written, conferences I attended, and reviews on *Rate My Professor*, for example. But there was plenty of personal stuff, too, like my wedding and divorce announcements and Emma's death notice. Luckily for me, I didn't grow up in the age of the internet, so some of my past required more than a Google search to exhume.

Though Audrey hadn't started a professional career at the time she disappeared, I figured there must be *some* information on her. I typed her name into Google and found shockingly little: a reference to her placing third in a high school track meet in Macungie, Pennsylvania and a link to a Prezi she had created for what looked like an environmental science class. I clicked on one of the components—there wasn't even a Works Cited or list of references that I could see, and I wondered why it wasn't password protected to prevent someone from ripping it off, but the quality was so low that it was unlikely anyone would.

I sighed and closed my laptop. *Nothing to see here, folks*. I still wasn't in the right mindset to complete my actual work. Jake was the detective, after all, not me. If he and his team hadn't found more on Audrey with their reserve of resources, why did I think I could? I was just a professor with basic internet skills.

*Because you* are *Audrey*, I thought, and immediately quelled that voice. I wasn't, but maybe I could've been. But I wasn't. I didn't like getting into these funks where the dark thoughts crept in. I needed something relaxing to watch on

TV to distract myself, a nice rom-com like "The Holiday" even though it was closer to Halloween than Christmas. I needed distraction.

I changed into my pajamas, comfy flannel ones printed with the Eiffel Tower that I had bought after purging my wardrobe of the silky negligees David used to request that I wear to bed. I was more of a flannel than a silk kind of girl, and I was fine with that.

Walking over to the fridge, I grabbed a half-full bottle of pinot grigio and poured a generous portion into a stemless glass. If I fell asleep on the couch watching a movie, I wouldn't mind. I dreaded the idea of lying in bed that night staring at my clock, unable to sleep due to the thoughts churning around in my head.

I lounged on the couch under a blanket, letting the well-known dialogue of the movie wash over me as the crisp, cool wine slid down my throat and began to work its magic, slowing my brain cells. But even young and charming Jude Law couldn't quash my dismay. I pictured Jake at the diner, grinning at me one minute and going back to Dragnet-mode the next. He would help Hadley, I knew it. Jake Ruiz had made it his mission to bring the perpetrator to justice. He wouldn't fail Hadley and her parents.

I remembered his hand on mine several days ago in my office and permitted myself to wonder what it might be like to have those dark eyes staring at me on a more regular basis.

A knock on my door brought me back to my senses. Norman leapt off my lap with an angry meow. I walked to the apartment door.

"Hello?" I asked. I didn't have a peephole and didn't want to risk cracking the door open, as I wasn't expecting anyone. My heart raced as I wondered who it could be. No one *ever* visited me, especially not after nine on a Friday night.

"Marissa. I wanted to apologize for the other day. For

being so abrupt when I left you at the diner." His voice sounded muffled, husky through the door.

I bit my lip in indecision. I was in pajamas, my face scrubbed free of makeup, with my hair in a sloppy, loose bun, and I'd already consumed two glasses of wine. And even though I wasn't a suspect or person of interest, I was kind of involved in the case. Was it appropriate? Was I ready to open that door and deal with whatever *this* was?

*Screw it.* I wanted this.

I opened the door. Jake had ditched his jacket and tie, and his white button-down shirt hung loose at the collar. He looked a bit rumpled, with a small stain over his pocket and heavy bags under his long-lashed eyes. "Hi," he said, his mouth contorting into a smile as he clocked my getup. "Can I come in?"

I nodded my head in assent and shut the door behind him.

"Hi yourself," I said, waving my hand over my face and body. "I wasn't exactly expecting you. And there's no need to apologize. I know you're giving everything you have to this case. I can't imagine doing what you do."

"Yeah. It can wear on a person." He closed his eyes tightly for a moment and then ran his hand over his face as if wiping off horrors he had seen. He looked like he needed sleep, a shower, and maybe a hug.

He looked like he was carrying all that weight alone.

I could relate. We were two lonely people, standing together in my apartment.

After a moment's hesitation, I placed my hand on his chest, feeling the heat of his skin through his shirt. An electric tingle rushed up my arm and through my body.

Jake reached for me and wrapped his muscular arms around my shoulders, holding me close. I melted into him, inhaling his scent, the ghost of his cologne as well as the whiskey on his breath. Tilting my face up to his, I waited until he put his soft, full lips to mine, tentative at first and then with hunger. His stubble grazed my face.

Jake's strong hands encircled my waist and then crawled up my pajama top, cupping my breasts. His lips moved to my neck, trailing kisses as I unbuttoned his shirt, wanting to feel his bare skin.

As Jake and I tugged off each other's clothes and inched toward my bedroom, I felt myself letting go of it all—the stress, the pent-up sorrow. Just for once, I stayed in the moment.

# CHAPTER 19

## THEN

"Congratulations, pledges. You've made it to Hell Week." Courtney's face was all angles and shadows beneath the dim light of the basement's single bulb.

The girls lay on the concrete basement floor, shivering in their new, clean uniforms, with their feet held six inches in the air—more of Abby's inventive lacrosse calisthenics that had slunk into OKB's rituals. They had been told to report to the function wearing fresh white T-shirts and boxer shorts underneath their clothes.

The expenses kept adding up, these garments plus all the cigarettes, mints, and bagged breakfasts for the sisters, not to mention all the cleaning and craft supplies. In the six weeks for which they had been pledging, they had spent a small fortune on paper towels and garbage bags alone. The demands on their wallets had been punishing, as the girls were tasked, at times with less than a day's notice, to satisfy some sister's whim by arriving at the happy hour decked out in silly costumes or with a new pledge banner.

The sheets, spray paint, puffy paint, Salvation Army clothes, felt decorations, and more cost money, a commodity of which Marissa had little, unlike some of her pledge sisters. Despite the attempts of bake sales and selling shots at parties, they weren't close to breaking even, especially with Hannah's disastrous pot brownies that hardly anyone ended up buying since they didn't cook right and smelled horrible. The money Hannah paid to a sleazy guy in her English class for the little bag of weed was another expense the pledges shared collectively.

Poor Hannah. Ever since the night a few weeks back when she'd wet her pants, she'd seemed a little different, standoffish. She had always been the first to laugh in group settings, but Marissa noticed that the smile rarely reached Hannah's eyes anymore. Marissa wondered how much Hannah recollected from that night, if anything, or if she woke up drunk and alone, reeking of urine, by herself in that very basement the next morning. Marissa couldn't remember much from that night, either, and none of the pledges really talked about it.

"That was kind of crazy," Kai had whispered into the phone later the next day. "I don't remember coming home."

"Me neither. And I slept through my class. I never skipped class before. Do you think Hannah's okay?"

"We'll know tonight," Kai had responded.

Marissa spent the next several hours sick with worry over Hannah, but she didn't pick up the phone to call her. Last year, a girl on her same dorm floor had gone to the hospital to get her stomach pumped after a night of reckless drinking. When Marissa was a junior in high school, a popular senior had choked to death on his own vomit while passed out at a party.

Marissa knew the risks, but she *still* did not call. The night had been so shameful, somehow, with only the few sisters yelling at them and making them drink to the point of blacking out. The pledges were used to being compliant, but that night was worse, crueler. If she didn't acknowledge how scary the situation had been—with none of the regular goofy fun and games, the dumb pledge songs and skits they had to create and perform—she could make herself think it wasn't that bad, just a bump on the road to sisterhood.

But then, Hannah showed up to the mixer with Sig Nu that night, looking like crap with puffy eyes and greasy hair. Marissa watched her shrug off Jessica's questions and stay silent and moody all night at the party. None of the sisters asked them to drink that night, even though some of the pledges nursed a beer, and Marissa wondered how many of the other sisters knew what had gone on in the basement, or if anyone actually cared.

All the sisters had pledged, after all, and maybe they were ensuring that it was just as hard for Marissa's pledge class as it was for them. Maybe they felt that it built character. Marissa hoped she would never become a sister who forced pledges to drink, but who knew? Maybe pledging would change her, and she'd want the pledges to suffer just as she had. If they didn't work as hard as she and her pledge sisters did, would she *want* future pledges to earn the sisterhood?

There hadn't been another incident like that after that awful night, just the normal punishments and trivial tasks. No matter how often they reminded each other to study the endless lists of facts about the current and past sisters, the pledge classes and family trees of Big Sisters and Little Sisters, someone would always forget something, and they'd all get punished with wall squats and pushups, yelled at about how they sucked and should try harder, or forced to drink.

Courtney must have been a schoolmarm in another life, as she liked assigning them writing when they messed up. They all needed to write "I will never miss an appointment with a sister" in their pledge books 150 times when Kai overslept and didn't show up at Amanda's apartment to do her nails as promised, and they had to write "fuck" five hundred times after Jessica had drunkenly sworn during a function. Marissa had taken over Jessica's task since she was too hammered to hold a pen at that point.

Even the regular day-to-day demands, the easy stuff like collecting the signatures and attending campus meetings, had become arduous. It all took time, and Marissa and her pledge sisters found themselves getting less and less sleep on the nights even when they weren't forced to stay up late drinking with the sisters... which meant that several of them had missed their classes and were dealing with plummeting grades on top of everything else.

So, when Courtney made her announcement that Hell Week had begun, the row of quaking girls breathed a collective sigh of relief that pledging was almost over. Angela had told them that the arrival of Hell Week was a good thing since it meant they were soon to cross the threshold into sisterhood.

"But before you reach heaven, you must go through hell. This week will push you in ways you may not have expected, both mentally and physically, so you can prove that you are worthy of becoming a sister of Omega Kappa Beta. Many have come before you to undergo these challenges. All of us, the sisters of Omega Kappa Beta, have endured. And we are confident that you will, as well, having come as far as you have."

As usual, Courtney's speech sounded scripted, and Marissa wondered if these words were all pre-written and passed down. This was one of many questions to which she hoped to learn answers after she was finally a sister.

Courtney paused a moment as the girls struggled, their legs trembling with exertion, their eyes squeezed shut to tap into their last bit of strength.

"You may lie down while the sisters anoint you with our letters. These letters are not yours to wear in public until after you earn the Rite of Initiation. For now, though, after having learned so much about the history and secret rituals of Omega

Kappa Beta, we are allowing you to wear our letters close to your heart and hidden from the rest of the world. Up until this point, you have not been allowed to wear our letters on your person except for your pledge pin. You've only been allowed to write them on your pledge book and your banner. But now you are inching closer to the full privileges of sisterhood."

Marissa felt a surge of pride for how far she'd come, even as she shuddered in this basement on her back. The truth was that she'd been writing them nonstop in secret, doodling the letters and symbols when bored in class. Her biology notes were full of them, which might have something to do with why her grade had been falling, that and how she'd skipped a few minor assignments after staying up late so often for a function.

But it would all be worth it, her canceled library shifts and reduced grades—she would soon earn the privilege of wearing the OKB letters out in the open. Everyone on campus, maybe even her old volleyball friends who barely said hi to her anymore, would know that she was a part of this organization. Everyone would know she belonged somewhere.

The sisters descended upon them like a swarm of wasps, armed with tiny bottles of red and black puffy paint, bending over the pledges and adorning them with the letters.

Angela bent over Marissa and smiled down at her. "You're almost there. I believe in you. You can do this. You're strong."

Marissa watched from her prone position as Angela concentrated, squeezing the bottle gently so a thin but steady trail of red paint oozed out, starting with the short arm of the omega and swinging up to create the O shape. She switched to black for the kappa and back to red for the beta.

Normally, the basement was an area for functions and heavy drinking, but the atmosphere seemed almost jolly as the sisters crouched over their human artwork. On this early

Sunday afternoon, no one was drinking, and someone had brought down a boom box. The cheerful, vapid music of Sugar Ray permeated through the often scream-filled basement.

"Nice work, Angela," Phoebe said, leaning over. "Your omega looks totally legit. Let me add something."

Angela backed away as Phoebe hovered over Marissa. She held her purple puffy paint bottle right by Marissa's face. "I brought my own so I could give you each a pansy. It was always my favorite sorority symbol." She uncapped and began outlining what Marissa assumed were petals, but she couldn't see since the sister was working up by her neck. "Pansies are purple, and purple signifies royalty," Phoebe continued in a low, singsong voice. "And pansies signify love and free thinking. The word pansy comes from a French word meaning 'thought.' *That's* why I appreciate the pansy. It is really, truly a special flower."

Marissa knew all of this from having memorized the sorority symbolism and history. Phoebe was so close that Marissa could smell the Sun-Ripened Raspberry Bath and Body Works lotion and fragrance on her skin. She didn't know if she should respond or not—Courtney hadn't instructed them, and Phoebe hadn't asked a question, so she stayed silent.

"I see you, Little Sister. You act meek and quiet, but I know you're a free thinker. You showed me that that night in the basement."

There had been many nights in the basement, but Marissa knew which one she must have meant. The problem was that she couldn't recall what all had occurred. Phoebe's quiet, ice-cold words cut right through the background chatter of the other sisters. "You let your guard down that night, when you got wasted. I saw the *real* Pledge Fugitive, and she's vicious."

Marissa felt her body heat rise in spite of the cool temperature. "I don't remember much about that night. If I offended you, Phoebe, I'm sorry."

Phoebe chuckled. "You didn't *offend* me, but you surprised me. I never expected you to talk back, but you just about bit Abby's head off when she suggested waking up Pledge Gonzo from her drunken stupor and making her drink. Abby was so shocked that she left you alone, believe it or not, for all her bluster. I didn't know you had it in you. Good on you."

Phoebe capped her paint and stood up, leaving Marissa to wonder what in hell she had done that night. And whatever Phoebe said, if she gained some begrudging respect for Marissa, she wondered if there would be repercussions that would bite her in the ass later that week.

---

"I THINK THEY'RE BACK," Janelle murmured as low voices and footsteps broke the silence above them. The pledges lay where the sisters had left them, hours earlier, so the puffy paint on their hell clothes would dry before the function.

The sisters had explained some basic rules of Hell Week which the pledges scribbled into their pledge books from their awkward positions on their backs. First, they would attend functions every night until the initiation. Second, they would sleep over every night at the sorority house in the basement, and study hall obligations would no longer be observed. Third, Hell Week could be a week or longer; it depended on how successfully the pledges handled their different trials. Fourth, now that they had donned their hell clothes, they were not to take them off for any reason until initiation, not even to shower, which they weren't allowed to do.

"I hope you're clean, girls," Courtney had said. "Baby powder works like a charm for the smell. And you *will* smell after a few days, but you still need to go to class. Try not to sit near anyone so as not to jeopardize the sorority. Look, we bought you some."

From her capacious handbag, she produced a few jars of Johnson & Johnson's. "It will soak up the grease. Blondes, you might even get away with putting it in your hair. Brunettes, sorry—it'll show up. Maybe wear a ponytail after it gets bad. But if one wears a ponytail, you *all* do, remember."

Wearing their hair the same way (up, down, half up, braids, whatever) was one of the many forced bonding activities the pledge class was required to observe for solidarity. This mandatory conformity contrasted sharply with the claims the sisters had made that the sorority prized uniqueness and individuality in its members.

The final rule of Hell Week was that it was their last chance to quit, for what the pledges would experience in the upcoming days was secret and reserved for future members of the sorority. While the sisters hadn't directly made threats about what would happen to a pledge who backed out at this stage, they intimated that it would be social suicide to stay at the college after quitting during Hell Week.

Part of the history the pledges learned was on cautionary tales: the pledges who came close but didn't make it, or sisters who got through the initiation but then left the sorority for one reason or another. These stories extended back almost as far as the sorority itself. Whether these anecdotes were true or not—Marissa and her pledge sisters couldn't tell—they were alarming for sure, both the details that were shared and the ones which remained unsaid.

Pledge Moonbeam quit talking to the sorority and her pledge sisters about a month into pledging. She didn't tell anyone what was going on or that she wanted to drop. She just stopped showing up to study hall hours and sorority gatherings. When her pledge sisters reached out to her, first by phone and then arriving at her dorm, she refused to talk to them, and no one knew why. Since Moonbeam demonstrated this disrespect to the organization that had fostered her, the sisters had no choice but to let their friends in other Greek organizations know what had happened. According to her roommate, who wasn't a sister but was friends with some girls in the sorority, Moonbeam stopped leaving the dorm except to attend class. She ended up transferring the next semester, but no one knew where.

Pledge Cornball, who went to the Dean of Students during Hell Week and reported Omega Kappa Beta for hazing, ended up getting pulled out of college by her parents and checked into rehab for drug addiction. Her pledge sisters—for her own benefit, they said—called Cornball's parents to let them know that she was struggling and that they were *concerned*. The subsequent Formal Board Hearing after Cornball's testimony was dismissed when the sorority leaders, upstanding young women who had started a community cleanup initiative and created a fundraiser to support the local women's shelter, explained that the poor girl's drug use may have caused their former pledge to imagine these delusions. Even without mandated punishments or community service, the sisters of Omega Kappa Beta hosted a campus talk on the dangers of drugs after this up-close-and-personal interaction with a friend who turned into a lying addict.

A girl named Josie, also known by her cartoon-based pledge name Pussycat, became a sister and contributing member of the sorority for two semesters, going to all the meetings and participating in activities even if she wasn't taking on any leadership roles. But after she slept with not one but two boyfriends of her sorority sisters, the sorority blackballed her. The sisters voted to oust her from OKB and seized her apparel with their letters. Josie left Blackthorn University and was never heard from again.

Through these different stories, one consistent message abounded: Being a part of the sisterhood equated to trust and belonging, and defying the sisterhood meant consequences. No one wanted to become another cautionary tale.

Therefore, when the sisters left them with the request not to move while they went off to live their lives, they listened. The pledges lay on their backs, talking here and there, thinking of their homework and the time they were wasting, and wondering what would come next.

---

"Tonight is a sacred time of bonding," Danielle began, her face illuminated over the single candle she held, the only source of light in the basement after turning off the bulb. The sisters slouched in folding chairs in a circle while the pledges sat upright, backs together, on the concrete floor which had only become colder as the day grew long.

While Courtney, as pledge mistress, ran most of the functions with Angela's support, there were times when one of the officers or senior sisters engaged in leading a function. As sorority president, Danielle took her turn more than others. "As you know, you may no longer quit without consequences. Tonight we will partake in our most secret ritual, which is aptly named the Ritual of Secrets."

Marissa cringed and began racking her brain. She'd always taken such cautions to keep her background private, not wanting to reveal her inner wounds for the pity or judgment of others. She hoped this would be another time for an embarrassing story she could share, not something painful.

Danielle's dark eyes slid over the pledges. "One way to prove your loyalty to each other is by telling something secret and personal about yourself, something you'd never want anyone else to know. I'm not talking about something little or

156

petty—I'm referring to the secret you keep in your heart, locked away. That deep, dark bit of meanness or ugliness you wouldn't want your enemy to have as ammunition against you. The Ritual of Secrets builds trust, and you need to trust each other. Trust is how we *know* we are sisters and that we have each other's backs. I know secrets about my pledge sisters"—she paused to nod at Phoebe, Abby, and Maribeth, the only girls who hadn't already graduated or dropped out from the Fall 1996 pledge class—"and they know mine."

Reaching for the candle, Abby rose from her chair and brandished a bottle of Chi-Chi's Mudslides. "It's hard to tell secrets, so we got you a bottle of that drink you like. We know that some of you have class early tomorrow, so this is a nice, easy drink to help take the pressure off but not get sloppy." Abby let her gaze linger on Hannah before continuing. "It's only, what, like two or three shots each? And half of that is probably milk or whatever. Nothing crazy. We'll give you an hour to drink the bottle of booze as a pledge class and spill your dirt. And we'll leave you alone. We'll go upstairs. But it's an important ritual. You can just drink out of the bottle. We didn't wanna bother getting out the shot glasses. If pledge sisters can share secrets, you can share spit, right? That's what I'm thinking." She handed the bottle to Janelle, who cradled it in her arms like an infant.

Angela passed out slips of paper and pens. "Sometimes our secrets are hard to tell. Write your secret on this paper first. Talk about your shared pledging experiences to remind each other how close you are. That's what helped my pledge class have the courage to share our truths, the ones we didn't wanna ever tell."

Someone turned the light bulb back on, and Abby blew out the candle. In a cacophony of scraping chairs and footsteps up the stairs, the sisters filed out and closed the basement door.

The pledges were alone again, backs to each other. They twisted around, not breaking the circle, coming face-to-face.

Truth. Secrets. Meanness and ugliness. No matter what they called it, Marissa's head pounded in protest, not wanting to divulge anything more.

Kai was the first to break the silence. "I think you already know my most embarrassing secret. And all of campus can take a good guess thanks to my pledge name. I mean, come on, Pledge Klepto doesn't leave much to the freakin' imagination." She reached for the bottle, unscrewed the lid, and took a sip. "At least this tastes good. They could've given us a bottle of shitty vodka or something."

"Yeah, Kai, but we *do* already know, so that doesn't count. They want more from us. Like, I don't know, if you boinked a professor or your friend's dad or something," Jessica responded, reaching out for the bottle and taking a deep drink. "Geez Louise, it still burns like a mofo. You'd think that all the drinking we've done in the past few weeks would've made it go down smoother. Shots still make me wanna hurl."

"And we've got plenty of practice with *that*, too," Janelle said, grabbing the Mudslides. The sisters had exchanged the candle each time someone talked, and the pledges, consciously or not, followed their lead but with the bottle. "I don't think I'll ever forget washing Hannah's chunks out of my hair after that one function. That was, like, horror movie-level disgusting. But, yeah, Jessica, I hear you. Something bigger than an embarrassing story. Maybe we should separate and write it down, and then come back when we're ready?"

Hannah spoke next after slurping the drink and widening her eyes. "My bad, Janelle. Anyway, liquid courage. That's what my dad always says. Yeah, chicas, let's split up for privacy."

More nods of assent, and the group scooted away from each other. Some of the girls wrote something down right away and came back to the circle to share the bottle, while others, like Marissa, hesitated.

She believed in trusting the sisterhood and understood that secrets bonded friends together. Would they still accept her, though, if she told her secret? She could always pick something else, something more innocuous, but would that fulfill her obligation?

In the quiet of the basement, the door creaked open. "Pledges! You have fifteen more minutes! Share your secrets and finish that bottle!" Courtney called.

Now or never. Marissa wrote down the shameful words she swore never to tell.

# Chapter 20

The sunlight streamed through my cheap Walmart curtains, waking me from what had been a deep slumber. No lying awake for hours, thinking about life, for once. I managed to sleep the whole night through. Well, I had been tired, exhausted, *after*.

I was still naked. Lifting the sheet just the tiniest bit so as not to wake him, I checked and saw that Jake was, too. A rush of warmth ran through my system as I thought back to the ways I had gotten to know his body the night before. He lay on his side turned away from me, his rhythmic breathing indicating that he was still sound asleep.

It seemed wrong to feel happy. Jake had only come into my life because Hadley died. We might have gone about our separate lives in the town of Blackthorn without ever meeting. If all were right in the world, Hadley would be in her dorm room right now working on Monday's assignment. But she was dead and buried, and Detective Jake Ruiz was in my bed au naturel.

I was thrilled to wake up next to a man, especially this

*Don't overthink it. It's not like last night necessarily meant anything to him.* The negative voice in my head, that one that told me I was never good enough or smart enough, rang loud and clear. Just because we had sex, a whole hell of a lot of sex, the night before didn't mean we were *together*. He could very well wake up, try to hide his regret, and hightail it out of my apartment before he'd even finished zipping up his pants. Maybe he made a habit of having one-night stands.

But was that all it was? It wasn't as if we'd just met—we'd known each other for close to two weeks now and had been building up to something. Still, it had been so long since I'd let my guard down even a little with a man, with anyone, really. Was I even *interested* in starting something with Jake? My warm feelings dissipated as I waited for him to wake up, my anxiety building.

His breathing sped up, and I felt the bed shift as he rolled over.

"Good morning," he said, cradling my face in his hand and placing his lips softly on mine, vestiges of last night's whiskey on his breath. As he trailed kisses down my neck and slid toward me, closing the gap between our bodies, my tension and negativity drained away, allowing space for joy. I wrapped my arms around his broad shoulders and let myself give in to the desire, to the fulfillment, to the now.

Afterward, we lay and looked at each other. I'd sat across from him several times, always with a table or desk in between us, and pretended not to notice those thick, black eyelashes and ever-present five o'clock shadow, but now I let my eyes wash over him and noticed new details, like the dark limbal rings around his brown irises and the scar on the corner of his hairline. I reached out and traced it with my fingertips.

"I played hockey in high school," he said. "Lucky I didn't get my teeth knocked out." He smiled, showing off his two full rows, and took my hand to his abdomen, where I felt a jagged, two- or three-inch-long raised scar. "Knife wound from when I tried to stop a domestic dispute. I had cuffed the man but wasn't expecting his wife, who I'd just saved, to have a go at me. Stupid of me, and it could've gone a lot worse, but I think of it as a reminder to watch my back and always be careful. Be prepared for the worst and don't trust anyone."

I let those words sink in for a second—he could have been describing my approach to interacting with people in the last several years. Maybe my whole life.

"We have very different careers," I said instead. "I think my biggest work-related problems are keeping up with my grading load and trying to reduce plagiarism. I can't imagine putting my life on the line like you do."

"Yeah, well, you put yourself out there in other ways, like how you connect with students, how you get them to see their potential. And being a cop is in my bloodline. My dad was police, too, and my grandfather before him back in Mexico. I grew up watching my mom kiss my dad goodbye each morning like it might be the last time. I think it just about broke her heart when I went into the police academy after college, even though that was always the plan."

He took a lock of my hair and twirled it around his finger. "What about you? Were your parents college professors, too? I guess we don't really know that much about each other."

"No. My mom was a waitress and my dad a mechanic. I grew up poor and was the first one to go to college." It seemed easy to say this now, in bed with Jake, in this protective bubble where I didn't need to think about proving myself to anyone.

"It became a whole thing with them. We never really had a close relationship, especially after I left for school. I almost never see my dad or my sister or nephews. My mom died when I was in college. Lung cancer." There—I let him see some of my red flags. I had no idea how much else he'd found out about me from the background check he performed before we ever spoke.

"I'm sorry to hear that. I spend a lot of time with my family, especially since my divorce."

*Divorce?* That was news to me. I glanced at his ring finger to see if an indentation was still there, to check if it was fresh.

He surprised me by laughing, and my face flamed with embarrassment at being caught. "I'm a detective, remember? It's been about five years now. I'm fine. It wasn't messy. We grew apart, and she moved across the country. We were only together a couple of years anyway. No kids or pets to make it complicated. And, just so I'm being forthright, I know you're divorced, too. My job is crazy and upsetting at times, but it doesn't mean I'm that stereotypical cop who's all messed up and can't separate life and work. I don't drown my sorrows in a bottle of whiskey every night. Last night was an exception. Last night was a lot of things, but I'm glad I showed up here, and that I took a Benadryl first." He pointed accusingly at Norman, who was sauntering over to the bed, a reminder that it was past his breakfast time.

Jake laced his fingers through mine, such an intimate gesture, but the chasm of our different lives and circumstances stretched between us. Even with Jake here, touching me, accepting me, I felt myself turning inward and pulling away.

"I *am* kind of messed up," I said, taking his hand down to feel my scar, the one that gave evidence that I was supposed to be a mother. I hadn't let David touch it. It was too raw then, mentally and emotionally, for me to let him, even though he may have needed it for his own healing. But that was then. "It's been a while now, but I still miss her. I came here, back to Blackthorn, for a fresh start, and it was going well, I thought, but now with Hadley—"

"We *will* find out what happened to her, Marissa. And I'm very sorry about your baby. I saw the fetal death certificate."

"Oh. Thank you." After so much exposure, I felt the need to cover up, so I shrugged on my pajamas, my back to Jake.

He took the cue and also began dressing, as well. I hadn't been with anyone since David. I'd put myself out there on a couple of dating apps and even engaged in some messaging with a few guys, but I couldn't summon the courage to show up to any of the proposed get-togethers. Once, I made it all the way to the restaurant and looked through the window to see the guy waiting expectantly. The thought of making small talk across a dinner table had been too daunting, though, and I didn't go in.

Yet here was Jake, this man I'd met because the investigation demanded it. I hadn't pretended to be a carefree woman with him; I didn't have to be. He walked into my office that day knowing some of my harsh truths and swaying on the cusp of others.

"I can make some coffee," I said, but as I turned, he was looking at something on his phone, and the darkness had fallen back over his face.

"I need to go. I'll call you later," he said. He skimmed his lips against mine and was out the door before I had time for any more questions.

# INTERLUDE

Rage fills my body, threatening to gnaw itself out from under my skin. I sense her bordering the truth, this woman, this sniveling coward. Such hypocrisy, how she demands justice when she herself has so much to conceal. But I cannot allow my wrath to control me, to expose me, or all of my efforts will come to naught. I must be purposeful, in control, to remain hidden, no matter my desire to scream and seethe.

*Calm.* I must stay calm, or I could lose everything. Candle magic will help, so I set my mood and intentions. I select a candle, a short white taper, pure and fresh, devoid of harmful vibrations. Grasping my athame, I carve CALM again and again into the waxy flesh and anoint the candle with grapeseed oil. After grinding sage and rosemary into bits with my pestle, I spread the mixture across the altar. Rolling the candle toward myself again and again, I dust it in herbs, inviting serenity.

The candle dressed and charged, ready for the spell, I set it into its pricket, surrounded with quartz crystals to amplify my intentions. Lighting the wick, I watch the flame dance and feel

Though my fury fuels me, I must keep it at bay and remain calm. For now.

# Chapter 21

## Then

The girls sat in a circle staring at each other. Jessica sighed. "Fine. I'll go first. My secret is that I cheated on the SATs. I hired some super smart girl who sort of looked like me to take it, and here I am on an academic scholarship. But *I'm* the one who's keeping myself here. I might've cheated to *get* that scholarship, but I'm *earning* the grades to keep it." She waited for the judgment of her friends, some of whom gaped at her.

"Damn, Jessica," Hannah said. "That's like, really heavy and totally unexpected."

Jessica shrugged. "I'm not proud of it. I used to have nightmares about getting caught. So now you know." Glaring, she met their eyes, daring them to challenge her. "And no one better fucking tell, and you each better give up something just as serious about yourself. If we are *truly* gonna be sisters, we need to trust each other." Having spilled her truth, she reached for the Mudslides bottle, but it was empty.

Janelle spoke up next. "I hooked up with my cousin. Like, not *hooked up* hooked up, but it happened last summer, and we've been all weird with each other since then. I'm hugging out, and it's horrible, and do *not* make any cracks about me being from West Virginia because I'm from *Virginia* and I really regret it." Her lower lip trembled and she looked down, away from her pledge sisters.

No one said anything. They understood the power of the circle of trust.

The next two girls shared their secrets. No one laughed or condemned. Each girl felt the weight of her words as she spilled them.

Marissa went last. "I had an abortion over the summer," she said. "I didn't know what to do. I needed to come back to college. I didn't want to become my mother." She had grown up in the shadow of her mother's "if onlys." If only she hadn't gotten pregnant after high school, she could have made something of herself. She could've met a better man than Marissa's father. Her mother let her know at every opportunity that Marissa's existence had derailed her life.

Marissa had been so stupid to let herself get carried away that night after work. She'd flirted a bit with Derek, the bartender, who was a few years older but not ridiculously so. As a waitress, she had to go to him for the customers' drink orders, and she had to admit she got lost in those blue eyes and dimples. He seemed so nice and funny.

When he asked if she'd like to come over to his apartment with a bunch of them from the restaurant one night after closing, she said yes. She enjoyed feeling like she was in the in-crowd, and her parents didn't care when she got home—they just wanted half of her tips.

Marissa wasn't reckless by nature, but everyone had a few drinks, and she didn't mind when Derek inched closer or slung his arm around her. She didn't mind when he suggested they go to his room, and she felt herself ignite with lust when he started kissing her. She didn't tell him it was her first time; that would have been embarrassing to let him know she'd waited so long only to give in to such a casual encounter. She thought it would be fine if he wore a condom, but she didn't actually check that he put it on. It was dark in the room, and she heard the rip as he opened a package, so why should she have worried?

Derek was nice enough afterward, she supposed, even though he hinted that it was time for her to leave at one point, and the next time she saw him at work he acted the same as always, like that night had never happened. So, a couple of weeks later when she realized that she was late, she knew she was on her own.

But that cold, sterile room was in the past. She felt Kai's arm around her and then Jessica's. She didn't realize she was crying until the tears dripped off her face, landing on her bare thigh.

"It's okay," Kai said. "It's all good. You did what you had to do. We love you."

Marissa looked up through blurry eyes at her friends. Secrets were safe in this circle.

The clomping down the stairs let the pledges know their time was up even before Abby's shrill announcement. Filing in, the sisters took their seats.

Courtney surveyed the pledges' grim faces and the pile of crumpled slips of paper. "Good. It looks like the group of you took this seriously. I'm proud of you ladies."

She reached into her pocket and procured a matchbook. "You might think that we were going to read your secrets and hold them against you, but we're not. In this sisterhood, we *keep* each other's secrets." She struck a match and dropped it on top of the papers, and all eyes watched as the flame took hold. The white papers coiled, sizzled, and blackened.

Phoebe, wearing her standard platform boots, stomped out the fire, leaving behind only ashes on the concrete floor. "The Ritual of Secrets is finished. You're done for the night."

The pledges curled up, shivering, on the concrete floor.

———

EACH NIGHT of Hell Week was similar to the last. Marissa struggled to complete as much of her homework as possible during her shifts at the library. Though allowed to take their schoolwork to the sorority house, the pledges were at the mercy of the sisters as soon as they walked through the door.

"Just a few more days, and it'll be over. It'll all be worth it," Kai said. The bags under her eyes looked like bruises, almost like she'd been in a fight and ended up with twin shiners. They had barely slept—not only was the basement floor uncomfortable, but they never knew when a sister might come downstairs to mess with them.

"We've all been through this," Angela explained. Janelle had started crying the previous night after Abby yelled in her face and called her worthless. "This is just part of proving yourself to the sisterhood."

It was poor consolation. Marissa understood the point of learning about the history and even making up silly songs. She didn't mind collecting signatures, pouring beers, lighting cigarettes, fundraising, or doing calisthenics. But the degradation —the screaming and humiliation—*that* she hated.

Most of the sisters were fine. They quizzed the pledges about Omega Kappa Beta facts and dispensed minor punishments here and there, like wall squats, but they didn't yell at anyone, and they didn't force them to drink. Tara, for example, was kind and funny, always checking in on how the pledges were doing and standing up for them if she thought another sister was going too far. But there were a few sadistic sisters who waited until the middle of the night to pay a visit to the basement. If they *were* getting initiated into the sorority soon, Marissa had a hard time imagining how she and her pledge sisters could make the leap to friendship with the sisters who had hazed them mere days earlier.

And the no showering thing was absurd. The pledges reeked of body odor, beer, and smoke. Marissa had started sitting all the way in the back of each classroom, away from her classmates, but she'd gotten a few looks of disgust as well as a couple of knowing smirks from members of other Greek organizations.

"Yeah, it'll all be worth it once we're in," she echoed hollowly to Kai.

---

ANOTHER FUNCTION, an easy one this time, on Friday night, the sixth night of Hell Week. Unlike a usual Friday, they weren't out at a frat party with multiple sisters—everyone had stayed in, and they had bought a keg of Coors Light, the good stuff compared to that repulsive Natty Light.

Most of the sisters and some of the pledges were half in the bag, but no one was forcing anyone to drink. Marissa nursed a beer to be social, but all she really wanted was to sleep, even if on this cigarette-butt-littered floor. Since the weekend was upon them, she knew she didn't need to wake up for class in the morning and was hopeful that the sisters would cut them a break for once. She would've fallen asleep in bio earlier if Kai hadn't pinched her to keep her upright.

"The theme of tonight's function is solidarity. We have all endured the trials of pledging before. So close to your sisterhood, when we know you must be exhausted, we want to remind you that we were once in your place," Courtney said. Rather than walking around clacking her heels, she sat relaxed in a chair. "We will each tell you our favorite memory of pledging, and then, by pledge class, we will perform one of the songs we created."

The pledges, sitting against the wall cross-legged, exchanged glances, waiting for the other shoe to drop, expecting they'd be told to do headstands or drink every time someone said OKB.

True to her word, Courtney began. "My favorite memory was when my pledge sisters and I had to drive to D.C. and act like we were French tourists—we each had to wear a beret, carry a baguette, and speak with an accent. It was stupid but kind of hilarious."

As she listened to the sisters' stories and saw the different pledge classes dissolve into fits of giggles as they sang ridiculous pledge songs set to the tunes of various popular music, Marissa's resolve softened. "Pledge," Fall '96's parody of the Talking Heads song "Blind," was particularly hilarious. The sisters were crying-laughing as they talked, looking back at their time pledging as something fun in retrospect. Even Abby shared a tender moment, and Marissa wondered if her tough act was for show. Maybe the real Abby was kinder than she seemed to be.

Maybe not. Abby was the one who woke them up that night, an hour after they lay down to rest.

"Come on," she said. "It's time to make some golden fucking memories."

———

THE WINTRY AIR pricked at their skin, but Abby said to wear only their hell clothes—no jackets or long pants. Courtney sat at the wheel of her Jeep, looking sober, at least.

"Hiya, girls! Get in the back so you don't pollute my car with your nasty funk! You'll keep each other warm."

The five pledges piled in on top of spread-out garbage bags, barely awake. There were two other sisters present, sitting in the back seat: Phoebe and Angela.

"Abby and I were thinking about our own pledging experience, and we thought back to a special function that we got to do, one that really bonded us for life. We don't think that the 'Kumbaya, let's all reminisce about when we pledged' bullshit that we did tonight was challenging enough for Hell Week. So we're off to the woods!" Phoebe clapped her hands after her spiel.

Marissa looked up at Angela, who was staring at all the pledges, checking in on them, perhaps. Despite the tribulations of the past week as well as their appearances and smell, everyone seemed to be okay, and no one appeared excessively drunk. At least the earlier function had been a fun and easy one. Marissa hoped that whatever they were doing next would be the same. She couldn't imagine that Courtney and Angela would go along with this if it was really bad. If it were just Phoebe and Abby, now *that* was a different story.

Hannah and Janelle had nodded off in the back despite Courtney blasting rap music as they drove on through the night. As the Jeep slowed to a stop, Marissa nudged the sleeping girls and suppressed a yawn.

Courtney waited as the pledges peeled themselves out of the back. "Okay, ladies. Time to prove you belong. Tonight you're participating in the Cliff of Life Ritual."

## Chapter 22

All day long, I tried not to be *that* woman, the one who checks her phone every thirty seconds for a call or text from a man. *He's at work trying to solve a* murder, I reminded myself. *He's not just blowing me off.*

I kept busy paying some bills, unearthing my stack of papers for a grading session but then putting them aside since I was too distracted, and finally going for a run to clear my head, which backfired since my mind kept flashing back to some NSFW images and sensations from the morning.

By the time I was home and showered, Jake still hadn't updated me on what made him run out of my apartment earlier, but I tried to take it in stride. It wasn't like he had to answer to me, and maybe he wasn't allowed to—classified police business or something. With Monday morning and the rest of the week looming in front of me, I finally tackled my freshmen comp papers.

Many of my students, especially the freshmen, complained that I wanted them to submit their work both online and as a hard copy, but there were elements I liked about each method:

If they turned their papers in online and I clicked a certain box on my end, every essay went through Turnitin, a plagiarism detector which exposed obvious cheaters and led to some important conversations and teachable moments with students who didn't fully understand how to use evidence from sources. But, as much as I tried to get on board with paperless essays, I felt too restricted typing my comments. Therefore, I still required printouts.

A pile of essays, even if they were only five pages each, was always daunting, let alone several piles. After refreshing my coffee, I set up my workstation with my favorite colorful pens. Grabbing my messenger bag, I removed the three binder-clipped bundles and set about alphabetizing by last name. I sighed, telling myself I would get the reward of a half-hour TV show and a single-serving size bag of kettle corn after I got through the first three.

While placing Browning behind Ballard, I noticed a piece of paper flutter to the floor and land facedown. My students were notorious for improperly stapling their papers, which drove me crazy, so I picked it up expecting to see part of an essay.

What I saw instead made the hairs on the back of my neck stand up.

STOP. One single word typed in huge Times New Roman font, centered in the middle of the paper.

Instinctively, I looked to the left and the right, as if whoever sent this message might somehow materialize in my apartment. This could be *any*thing. Maybe someone grabbed this random paper from the printer and accidentally turned it in with their essay. It had happened before—I got math home-work and all kinds of nonsense. Once I even received a field trip permission slip for the child of one of my nontraditional students.

But if this was intentional, if this note was meant for me, then stop *what*? With Jake fresh on my mind, I imagined his ex-wife targeting me and telling me to stay away from her man. Then again, I collected these papers on Thursday and Friday, before Jake and I had crossed the line from a professional to personal relationship.

The logical explanation wasn't a pleasant one. Someone wanted me to stop meddling in Hadley's murder case. How would they *know*, though, what I had found out?

Off task yet again, I agonized over possible answers. Maybe someone had seen the detectives and Hadley's parents coming to my office, or Jake arriving at my apartment. Maybe someone knew that I'd been to Hadley's funeral. However, that seemed standard since she was my student—even the president of the university was there.

How would anyone know that I'd scoured her papers for clues, or that I'd done a deep dive on the internet about the Poppies? I hadn't even found anything, so why would anyone think I was getting close?

Unless I *was*.

If my paranoia were correct, and someone was asking me to stop digging around, the next questions were *who* they were and *how* they managed to plant this paper. And maybe the most important question: *why*?

I pictured Peter Browning, the student whose paper was in my hand when the note fell out. A quiet young man who never missed a class and turned in each assignment, a rarity amongst my freshmen, he seemed an unlikely suspect.

Then again, lots of us were hiding dark secrets. I just had to look in the mirror to remember that. Peter didn't make sense, though. The only clue I had helped Jake turn up was Hadley's involvement with the Poppies, and Peter was a *guy*. As far as I knew from the skeleton of evidence we'd unearthed, the Poppies were a sorority. I knew of some co-ed fraternities, mostly honors organizations tamer than the average frat, but Hadley had asked me my opinion on sororities, meaning girls only; I was certain.

So, not Peter. Even if someone had tasked him with giving me the note, he would have been an idiot to incriminate himself by placing it next to his own essay. It would've been easy enough for a student to wait for the stack to grow and then slip it in.

In fact, someone could have accessed my bag when I *wasn't* in class. I used to live in Baltimore, so I wasn't so naïve as to leave my belongings out in the open at a restaurant or public bathroom and turn my back. Truth be told, though, I wasn't always on guard. If I was in my office at work, getting things done or conducting office hours, I definitely left the door ajar and my office unattended when I needed to run downstairs to use the copier or pop over to Candace's office for a quick chat. I locked up if I was headed to my classroom or across campus, but my office *was* open at times if someone was watching and waiting for their moment.

And maybe someone *was*. I thought back to that night when I thought I heard a click in the stairwell. If someone was stalking me, it was likely they could get away with walking right into my office without any suspicion. Not some home-less person or escaped convict—a student, or maybe someone who worked at the university.

But was this note really a threat? Was I acting crazy? There was one person I needed to tell, so I had to buck up and stop being weird about it. If I called, Jake might think I wanted to go on a date, or, even worse, talk about my feelings. Not that I *wasn't* up for that, but I'd let him know why I was contacting him.

I sent him a quick text: *I found a strange note in my bag. I don't know if it's a threat.*

Okay. His move on both fronts, the investigation as well as

the romance, if that's what this was and not a fling. I sat back and waited. Unbidden, as always, a memory formed of another time I'd felt the potential of danger tapping its fingertips against my neck.

# CHAPTER 23

## THEN

By instinct, even in her frozen, trance-like state, Marissa had pulled her hand away instead of holding on. But, the spell now broken, she was catapulted into panic mode.

This could *not* be happening. Marissa's mind jumped to conclusions, to the worst-case scenario.

"Kai? Kai? Are you okay?" All the girls were looking over the cliff's edge, trying to see where Kai had fallen. Marissa had felt her wobble—they'd all been shivering hard in the cold—but the stumble and fall had happened so fast. And then that bone-chilling shriek.

Courtney's eyes went wide in the moonlight. "Kai? Call out if you can hear us! We're coming for you!" It was probably the first time Courtney had called Kai by her actual name in the six weeks of pledging; it was always Pledge Klepto until that very moment.

"Oh my God, oh my God, oh my God," Angela chanted before bursting into noisy sobs. "What if she's not okay? This was supposed to be a bonding experience!"

Courtney shone her flashlight. "Shh. Let me concentrate. I can't see her." She tested a ledge near the cliff's edge and pulled her foot away. "It's too steep here. We need to go back down and around. We don't have any time to waste. Let's go."

Several of the girls had joined Angela in weeping. "She isn't answering! What if she's dead?" Hannah cried, all earlier traces of tipsiness gone.

Abby stepped forward. "Shut the fuck up! Don't say that until we know what's going on! Come on." She grabbed Hannah by the arm and followed Courtney's lead, but Marissa read the fear in the older girl's eyes.

Marissa trailed behind, thoughts screaming and pounding in her head. She pictured her friend splayed out on the rocks below, unmoving. She tried to push the images away and focus on the now: Maybe Kai would be okay. Maybe she was knocked out but otherwise unharmed. The cliff didn't go straight down—she could be stuck, and they could get help.

"Maybe one of us should go for help now," Jessica said, seeming to read Marissa's mind. "Courtney, you have a car phone in your Jeep, right? Someone should call 911. We can save Kai if we break up and make this a team effort."

Courtney, always so sure of herself, hesitated, her voice faltering, barely more than a whisper. "I don't know. I don't know *what* we should do. I'm scared."

It was Phoebe who spoke up, her voice clear and steadfast. "No one's going anywhere. We need to find out what we're dealing with, and then we'll decide what to do. I need all of you to understand that, whatever we find, it has the power to change the outcome of our lives. *All* of our lives."

Marissa felt a chill in her veins that had nothing to do with the freezing air around her.

AFTER A SILENT TEN-MINUTE trek through the woods that seemed like a lifetime, they reached the bottom of the cliff. Kai was most certainly *not* okay.

She had fallen straight back and lay spread-eagled on a boulder, her arms out as if she were making a snow angel, her neck cocked to one side, her eyes open and sightless.

Hannah pushed through. "I'm a nursing major," she reminded them. She reached out for Kai's wrist.

Her next words, choked and weak, were nearly swallowed by the night. "I don't feel a pulse."

Marissa rushed to her friend's side. She wasn't a hugger, but she was drawn to her. She wanted to hold her in her arms and give her comfort if there was anything left of Kai—if she was still fighting.

Phoebe shot out her arm, clotheslining her. "Don't touch her. We need to be careful. We can't leave any evidence."

"Evidence? Phoebe, what the fuck are you talking about?" Jessica said. The pledge versus sister hierarchy didn't matter anymore. "Kai is my *roommate*. This is an *accident*. We need to get help *now*, at least call someone, even if it's too late."

Her face drawn, Phoebe stared down her companions. "Don't you understand? The cops won't look at this as an accident. It's midnight in October *in the woods*. This is hazing. We're all liable."

"Fuck you, Phoebe. *You're* liable." Hannah spoke up, pointing at the sisters. "And you, and you, and, sorry, Angela, even you. *You're* the ones who've been hazing *us*. *We're* not getting in trouble for anything. As if."

Hannah looked at her pledge sisters, those who remained. "Let's go to the Jeep and call 911 now, even if we have to pry the keys out of Courtney's hands. Kai deserves better than this!"

Courtney, stricken, peered at Kai's bloody, broken body. "I'm so sorry. I'm so, so sorry. We took part in this function, also, and we were fine! I promise you, we were all fine!" She collapsed onto the ground and put her head between her knees, her breaths fast and ragged.

Marissa heard the jangle of keys coming out of Courtney's pocket and made a move to grab them, but Phoebe snatched them away.

"I don't think everyone understands our situation here. *Why* did Kai fall? All of *you* were holding hands. If you were there for each other, *really* there, you should have caught her! Four girls can hold up one. Like it or not, we're all going down for this. We're all part of what happened, and, if we call the cops, we're *all* in trouble."

She stepped out, in front of Kai's body, and shone the flashlight so everyone could see. "If we don't work together here, every single one of us will be in serious legal trouble— hazing, neglect, giving alcohol to an underage person. Do all of you remember that my dad's a lawyer and I'm a pre-law major? We will *all* be expelled and probably go to jail, and we will *all* have a record. Do you understand me?"

Phoebe's voice rose in volume over the howl of the furious wind. Even dressed in a jacket, she was shaking now, and Marissa wondered if it was with cold, panic, or rage. Perhaps all three.

"So, you don't want us to call anyone? You want to leave her here? Alone in the woods? Are you insane?" Courtney was screaming now. "These girls are our *responsibility*! They're supposed to become our sisters!"

"And I'm supposed to go to law school, and you're supposed to get married next year! What about us? It's too late for Kai. What about us?" Phoebe demanded.

"What about *her*?" Marissa said. "How can we live with ourselves if we leave her?"

Angela stepped forward, positioning herself next to Phoebe. "Phoebe's right. I feel terrible for Kai, but we need to think of ourselves, too. She's gone. She doesn't have a future, but we do. Even if we don't go to jail, there's gonna be consequences—fines, getting kicked out of school, whatever."

Angela stared into Marissa's eyes, pleading. "Where would *we* go? We're both here on need-based scholarships and don't have the money to hire criminal defense lawyers. I *need* to finish school. I can't go back home and work at Burger King all my life. Kai would get it."

Janelle moved forward next. "I agree. I already have a criminal record. You guys know—stupid marijuana charge. But something else, something like this, would destroy me for sure. I don't wanna risk it."

One by one, the girls joined the row, until it was nearly a circle around Kai's body. They linked hands as Marissa watched, not joining them.

Marissa thought back to how Kai had always been there for her. Kai had shown her that real friendship existed after her rejection by the volleyball girls the previous year. She had sought out her company and made Marissa feel appreciated. And now Kai was gone, and Marissa was partly to blame. If only she'd held on when Kai had stumbled. But she hadn't.

Marissa imagined a life where she was expelled from college and had to go back home to the trailer park—that is, if she didn't go to jail.

When Marissa walked forward, joining the others, she completed the circle.

---

"YOU'RE sure she's dead, right?" Abby asked, nudging the corpse with a stick.

"I'm not a nurse yet. I'm only a sophomore. But we were shown how to take a pulse, and I don't feel anything. And her eyes are open." Hannah jogged in place to warm up.

"Here's what I'm thinking. We can't leave her like this, in her hell clothes with our sorority letters. It'll go right back to us when the cops find her body. Angela, you're about the same size. Take off your clothes, and we'll put them on Kai. You put on hers," Phoebe commanded.

Angela gaped at her. "You want me to put on her *hell* clothes and give you my jacket and clothes? Her *blood* is on her clothes!"

Courtney nodded, her earlier hysteria vanished. "I agree with Phoebe. If she's found, we're finished. It has to look like she was here on her own, not as a part of pledging, or it will lead right back to the sorority, back to us."

"Why would she be here alone after midnight?" Jessica asked. "And didn't you guys have to turn something in saying who the pledges are? She'll be tied back to us no matter what. She's my roommate! I know her parents!" Having remembered this, Jessica burst into fresh tears.

"Jessica, what happened here is a tragedy. A girl's life has ended tonight, but does that make it right that all of our futures have to end? We need to protect ourselves. Strip, Angela," Phoebe ordered. "I'll buy you another goddamn jacket. I'll take you on a fucking shopping spree. I don't care. Whatever. But we need to do this *fast* and get back to the house before anyone wakes up and figures out that we're gone. We were *never* here, understand? Kai sneaked out during the night, and no one knows where she went. That's what we'll say to the other sisters."

Angela disrobed, letting each article of clothing fall into a pile on the leaf-covered ground. When she got down to her bra and underwear, she clutched her arms over her chest, shivering.

Courtney stood over Kai's prone form and began removing her hell clothes, slowly pulling her shirt up and around her head, gently, like she was taking care of a newborn baby. "I'm so sorry, Kai," she said, her voice breaking. "We'll keep you warm now."

Marissa stepped forward, shaking as much from shock as from the frigid air. "I'll help you. She was my best friend."

Marissa and Kai had never used that term—it sounded silly, juvenile, like they were back in junior high with those stupid half-heart BFF necklaces. But that's what they had become to each other, and Kai's absence burned like a hole in her soul. Phoebe nodded her consent and handed Marissa her gloves to wear.

The thought of touching a dead body had always terrified Marissa. As a teenager, her dad had asked her to clean up a dead rabbit in their yard that had been killed by the neighbor's dog, and she'd broken down in tears at the horror of moving the tiny, rapidly stiffening corpse. But this was Kai. She *had* to.

With Courtney's help, she slid Angela's shirt over Kai's limp head and shoulders and pulled up her jeans. They placed the coat on and zipped it up. The others watched in silence.

"I don't want to wear her clothes," Angela said, her teeth chattering. "I'll just stay like this."

"We have to take them, though, and burn them. We need to get rid of any evidence that points back to us." Phoebe's voice was a whisper in the darkness.

"But why would she be *here*, by herself? The other sisters know she was at the house earlier. When someone finds her, the girls will put it together." Abby became shriller, her lisp more pronounced, as she worked through the scenario. "Maribeth was there with us, Phoebe, when we did the Cliff of Life Ritual back when we were pledging. None of the others have done it, so they wouldn't think it, but she did, so she'll guess. Why else would Kai be in the woods? Once they find her and call the cops, it'll all come crashing down on us."

"Then maybe we shouldn't let them *find* the body," Hannah said. "All we know is that we went to sleep and Kai was there, but we woke up and she was gone. That's the story. A missing person could be anywhere, but a body could point back to us." She looked out at the rest of them for affirmation.

Marissa found herself nodding along with everyone else. *This is what they* had *to do for self-preservation, right?* She imagined Kai's parents getting the news that their daughter was missing. The only thing worse than finding out she died would be never knowing what happened to her. Still, what was the alternative? Eight lives had to count more than one. They *had* to do this—they had no choice.

"But what do we *do* with her? We don't even have a shovel. We can't bury her," Janelle said.

"Think. We're in the woods. There has to be a little cave or something, right? If she's found eventually, it could be okay. We just can't have that happen for a while, to give us some space. She could've run off with some guy or something. He could've brought her here, she fell, and he hid the body so he wouldn't get in trouble."

Phoebe paced up and down in the clearing. "We need to leave ASAP. Start looking now. Stay in groups of two, no one alone." She grabbed Marissa's arm, pinching hard. "You're coming with me."

*This is real. This is happening.* Marissa wished it was a nightmare, that she'd wake up on the basement floor with nothing more than a sore back. But Kai was dead, and they had agreed to hide her body to save themselves.

"We have to do this. We don't have a choice," Phoebe said once they had walked away from the others. "I know how close you two are. *Were.* Kai wouldn't want our lives to be ruined."

"I know," Marissa said, still feeling like a traitor. She thought back to the numerous acts of kindness Kai had committed in their friendship, small things like saving Marissa a seat at lunch, and bigger instances where Kai had stood up for Marissa during functions and gotten in trouble herself. "I'm not going to tell anyone. You can trust me."

Phoebe stared straight ahead, her eyes darting back and forth over the expanse of landscape. "I'm not worried about you. You're smart—you get it. You understand what could happen if anyone found out. But do you trust *them*?"

"It's not like we have a choice," Marissa answered, almost echoing Phoebe's words. "We need to trust each other, or we're all going down."

Her mind flashed back to that Ben Franklin aphorism she had read in high school: *Three can keep a secret if two of them are dead.* But there were *eight* of them in total, seven other girls who might not be able to live with the guilt of what had happened in the woods. Seven other girls threatened *each* of their futures. It was Phoebe's idea not to call for help and Hannah's idea to hide the corpse; *they* wouldn't tell. But what about the others?

Her thoughts were broken by the sound of Abby's breathless voice. "Hey! We found a place for the body!"

# CHAPTER 24

"Aren't you going to dust it for fingerprints?" I asked. The patronizing glance Jake gave me assured me he would not. "It's not really like what you see on TV." I caught the hint of a smirk on his lips. "The note might be nothing. If someone was trying to scare you, they'd probably be more direct, like 'Stop looking into Hadley's death or you're next.' But 'STOP' by itself is super vague. Why even bother with a note? Maybe it was from a student and meant 'Stop giving us so much homework.'"

"Ha, ha. Maybe they *wanted* to make me paranoid. Maybe they wanted me to question whether this was nothing or if it's something, just to rattle me but not make me do anything about it. Maybe a bigger threat comes next if I don't stop." I didn't love his tone.

He'd texted back pretty quickly after I got in touch, not with a call or questions but a simple *I'll come over after work if that's okay?*

Ugh. I was horrible at navigating this. He sounded less like a homicide detective after a lead and more like a man who wanted to make a booty call. I couldn't decide which role was more palatable.

Jake got up from the kitchen table and stood behind my chair, placing his hands on my shoulders and starting to rub them. As soon as I felt his powerful grip, some of the tension drained out of my body.

"Marissa, you *have* been helpful with the investigation by giving Welch and me information about Hadley's personality and finding that clue about the Greek letters that led me to the Poppies, but you are *not* part of the investigation. You need to let my partner and me worry about the case. Hadley's death is tragic, and I know you cared about her. But you told me yourself that you've lost a number of former students, and you think of them sometimes and feel sad, but you don't dwell on their deaths. Let *me* worry about Hadley's death. It's my job. *Your* job is to work with the students you still have. Unless you can think of anything else the police need to know about Hadley, your role in this investigation is over."

He was right, and his voice sounded gentle, but it still felt a little condescending. Wriggling from under Jake's grasp, I turned to face him, to look into those deep, dark eyes and try to help him understand how I felt.

"Look, I *know*. I know I'm not on your super sleuth team. But you also can't expect me to just flip a switch and move on. Every time I see that empty desk, I'll think about the fact that Hadley's gone. The funeral wasn't even a week ago. I'm not over it, and you shouldn't expect me to be. I only knew her for a few weeks, but I cared about her. Her death is *haunting* me."

Jake sat back down and placed his hand over mine. "I'm sorry if I seem cold. I've had to shut myself off from feelings, at times, so I don't get attached to the victims in a way that could compromise my ability to do my job. I know you cared about her. I just hate to see what this is doing to you. I *care* about you, Marissa."

My pulse started racing as my skin burned with frustration. I pulled my hand away from his. "What *is* it doing to me? It's not like I was all that great *before* this happened. You didn't even know me then, and you don't know me that well *now*. If anything, the idea of being able to help find Hadley's killer is giving me a purpose. It makes me feel like I'm doing something right for once."

As soon as I said it, I was struck with the realization of why uncovering Hadley's killer was so important to me. I hadn't done the right thing when Kai fell, and I'd never moved past it. Nothing would make up for what happened in the woods on Hell Night all those years ago, but maybe I'd feel some small sense of redemption if I could help Hadley's parents find a sense of closure—something Kai's family never received.

Jake nodded, his eyes downcast during this dressing-down. I half-expected him to continue with some cop-speak to reinforce that I needed to keep my nose out of police matters, and I half-worried that he'd question me about *when* I didn't do the right thing in the past.

Instead, he paused, his brow furrowed, seeming to consider his words before speaking. "You're right that I don't know you that well, but I'd *like* to know you better," he said, making eye contact. "Last night—and this morning—meant a lot to me. I'm not really a casual guy. But, if this isn't something you want or can deal with, I can handle it. Just tell me to go, and I'll go."

My annoyance fizzled out as quickly as it flared up. "I don't want you to go, Jake. I guess I feel left out with you having information about the case that I don't. But I get that I'm only her professor and not a family member or anything, so I don't have the right to know everything."

I let my words hang there for a moment.

"When you ran out of here earlier today, it made me

wonder what was going on. Maybe you discovered something that I could shed light on as a former member of a sorority or as someone who understands the intricacies of higher education. All I know is that you know cop stuff, but I have insight into things that you don't." I crossed my arms, not exactly challenging but also not relenting.

Jake pushed his chair out like he was going to get up, but then he tipped his head forward and held it in his hands for a moment before meeting my eyes again. "There's some new information that may be important to the case, and maybe you *can* help figure it out. Hadley's parents paid me a visit today. That's why I ran out of here this morning. They had taken her belongings from her dorm room when they came to campus the same day you met them, but they only began looking through it later, after the burial. One thing at a time, they told me. They said they were in such a state of shock that they just grabbed everything the roommate said was Hadley's and threw it in boxes. They took everything without looking."

My pulse raced with anticipation, wondering what on earth they had discovered. "Didn't you guys look through her stuff, though? Wouldn't you have already found whatever it was that's so intriguing?"

I received an arched eyebrow in response, but he continued anyway. "We were looking for things that could be linked to her death. Drugs and drug paraphernalia, along with any personal items that could indicate relationships, good or bad, with people. We read through all her notebooks, searching for a diary, something like that. We weren't looking for *this*."

"Oh my gosh, just tell me already, Jake. I'm on the edge of my seat."

"The Parkers opened up this big jewelry box they'd given Hadley when she was a kid, one of those with a ballerina on top that you wind up and it plays a song. One of my guys had been through it but didn't think it was important, since it contained what seemed like random things: some little jars of essential oils as well as one that had dirt, a candle, a feather, a metal cup, some shiny rocks. Kind of weird, but my ex was into essential oils, and my one nephew had a rock collection. We thought they might be some sentimental items Hadley took to college with her to feel connected to home. But her parents got all freaked out. They said she'd never collected rocks, and the essential oil thing was new to them. Mrs. Parker said her sister used them, but Hadley never showed any interest.

"And when she was showing me this stuff and telling me about it, I remembered something I saw in the coroner's report and photographs that I didn't think anything of at the time. Hadley had a tattoo on her ribcage, one that didn't look professional—a homemade one. But tons of college kids have tattoos, right?"

I nodded. "Not so much when I was in college, but, yeah, I see visible tattoos on a good number of my students. What was it?"

He reached into his pocket and grabbed his notebook. He drew a star and then a circle around it. "A pentagram, or, technically, a pentacle—a word I learned today. I haven't been involved in any cases with satanic cults, but I've read about some, and I know that this sign can be associated with devil worship. I grew up super-Catholic and was told to stay away from *anything* to do with the occult. Then again, I know that people have tattoos of all kinds of things on their bodies, like skulls and animal heads, so the pentacle didn't really stand out. But then, with all that weird stuff the Parkers found, I made the connection.

"It looks like Hadley was into some sort of witchcraft. Or Wicca—again, I just looked this up today, so I'm no expert, but those objects seem to be fairly common, so much so that you can even buy a witchcraft beginner's kit from Amazon or Etsy. Some of these are supposed to represent the elements: earth, air, fire, water. And all this could be completely harmless, some weird thing she was exploring, you know? But we're grasping at straws here. I might've wasted hours of my day today researching the Wiccan religion for nothing."

He sighed, showing that this was getting to him even though he said he tried to cut off his emotions. "Everything that I found about Wicca suggests that it's about belonging to a group, and that's what sororities seem to be like, too. My gut tells me it's all connected. What if the Poppies were practicing witchcraft and something went wrong? I can't help but think about how Hadley was pregnant, and how the baby was— taken away."

Jake ran his fingers through his hair again, and I wondered if he was treading softly because of my own lost baby. "With your background, your scholarship, do *you* know anything about witchcraft? Everything I found today on Wicca seemed to be pretty innocent, like it's just the religion these people practice, and it's more about loving nature than worshiping Satan or anything like that. But I keep wondering if it's darker."

"Oh," slipped out before I could get my bearings together. "I'm an expert on Poe, not witches, and he didn't directly write about witchcraft. There are some tie-ins with ritual magic in some stories, but no actual *witches*. Do you want me to get into all that?" I didn't want to give him a lecture on metempsychosis, where a soul migrates into another body, if that's not what he was after. "I don't know much about witchcraft except what I've seen in movies I watched as a teenager, really. I'm sorry I can't be more helpful."

He didn't seem to hear me. "I asked the Parkers if they knew about Hadley's tattoo. They didn't, but I bet that's nothing too unusual for parents. I *told* them about the tattoo,

Marissa. I don't know if I should've, but I thought they might know something that could help the case. But all I did was upset them. I think I made them feel like they didn't know who their daughter was. And I felt like I was tattling on her, you know?"

Jake's eyes stared not at me but through me. He stood up, pushing in his chair and giving me a quick kiss on the lips, all his movements as frantic as the waves of unrest he radiated. There would be no follow-up sleepover tonight. "I'm sorry, but I have to go. I need to do some more research on this."

"I understand," I said. Leading him to the door, I tilted my face to his for one more kiss. I walked back to my office, past the STOP note with its command, one I was choosing to ignore.

# CHAPTER 25

## THEN

It looked like an animal's den: a hollow area under a tree, far from any of the hiking trails. *Way* off the beaten path.

"We'll have to clear out some of the debris first," Courtney said, already dragging out a broken branch and dead leaves. "I think she'll fit, though."

"Good thing she's tiny," Abby said. "We'll still need to wedge her in."

"We've gotta hurry before rigor mortis sets in," Hannah said. "We'll have to, like, kind of fold her."

Marissa worked like an automaton for the next several minutes, scooping out loose dirt without thinking, preparing to conceal the body of her closest friend. Jessica and Janelle, with their athletic builds, were elected to carry Kai when it was time, and they did so with grace, sliding her into the opening. There was a sickening thud as they pushed her down deeper.

"It's not enough. Someone could still come by. We need to cover the hole. Let's see if we can move that rock." Phoebe pointed to a mid-size boulder which the girls then pushed and heaved until it was nearly in front of the hole.

"Wait. Before we close it off, we need to say a prayer or

something for Kai," Angela said. "We need to do *something*. Should we write her name on the rock?"

"Absolutely not," Janelle said. "Then they'll know someone was here."

"Let's all say something quietly. Let's have a moment of silence," Courtney said.

"Make it snappy. It's time to say goodbye. We need to get back," Phoebe ordered.

*Goodbye, friend. I am so sorry*, Marissa thought, and she helped push the boulder to fully camouflage the hole.

---

BACK IN THE JEEP, even with the heat blasting, the pledges couldn't stop shivering.

Phoebe doled out instructions, staccato, to the group. "I'll dispose of her clothes. Courtney, drop us off at the house. Then, drive to Angela's dorm for some clothes for her. Leave her in the car while you get them, or let her borrow yours while she gets new ones. Pledges, when we get back, be as quiet as possible and sneak downstairs. Get some sleep. The sisters are coming to the house at seven a.m. to wake you up for the Rite of Initiation ceremony. Act happy, act surprised, and act confused that Kai isn't here. No one saw anything; no one understands where she went. She didn't say a word to anyone.

"This is a new sisterhood we're in now—the eight of us. We *cannot* tell anyone what happened in the woods tonight. If one of us breaks, we all fall. Does everyone understand? If one person tells, we are all *fucked*. Do you hear me? I know this is scary. But we can't tell anyone, and we shouldn't even talk about it again to each other. Kai left during the night. Say it with me. It's what we'll need to tell the school and the cops when they question us, and they *will* question us. Kai left during the night."

"Kai left during the night," the girls chorused, and then they continued the drive back to Blackthorn in silence.

*We're getting initiated in the morning*, Marissa thought. This big thing she thought she cared about, earning her letters, had become bereft of meaning. Everything had changed in the last few hours. She leaned her head against the side of the Jeep and tried to erase all she had seen, felt, and done that night.

# Chapter 26

No matter what Jake said, no matter how easily he could explain away that note, the meaning seemed clear: Someone knew that I was sticking my nose into things, and they felt threatened. If I retreated, I'd learn nothing, but there was a chance I could flush out a new clue if I kept going.

I had so much to process since I had last taught on Friday. As students filed into my class that Monday morning, I smiled and greeted them while scanning, as I had the past few days, for the telltale poppy flowers on backpacks. It was unlikely that I had another of the Poppies' pledges in my caseload—if pledging was even still occurring—but I searched all the same, walking through the rows and checking in as my freshmen completed their group work.

I'd phoned it in for the comp classes, anxious for my Poe class that evening, thinking about what I had planned.

In my class of only twenty-three remaining students, since Hadley was gone and another student had withdrawn, it was even less plausible that one of the Poppies was right under my strange details about their professors, and they posted ridiculous amounts of information, anonymously or not, on social media. What we were doing in class that day was bound to get students talking.

If witchcraft was connected to what happened to Hadley, whether with the Poppies or not, then someone was sure to hear about my class that day. I felt that double-edged sword of excitement and dread I used to feel before running a race.

"Hi, everyone. Today we're going to talk about rituals in Poe's stories. Before we get into dealing with the reading for today, 'The Cask of Amontillado,' I want to provide some information on ritualism in Poe's stories prior to when he moved to Philadelphia. Get ready to take some notes."

I switched on the projector and started the PowerPoint, explaining metempsychosis and giving a little background on the stories "Metzengerstein," "Morella," and "Ligeia." None of these involved actual witchcraft, though, so I had to be more obvious in my quest to draw out the author of the note, if, in fact, he or she existed.

"There's one scene in 'Ligeia' where Rowena, the narrator's new bride, lies dying in her chamber before Ligeia takes over her body. Remember the colorful rooms in 'The Masque of the Red Death'? The description of the room is important here, as well." I read Poe's words to them:

*The room lay in a high turret of the castellated abbey, was pentagonal in shape, and of capacious size. Occupying the whole southern face of the pentagon was the sole window — an immense sheet of unbroken glass from Venice — a single pane, and tinted of a leaden hue, so that the rays of either the sun or moon, passing through it, fell with a ghastly lustre on the object within.*

"Does this sound like the narrator's creating a romantic setting for Rowena, his new wife? Of course not. He's still obsessed with Ligeia."

I drew a pentagon on the dry erase board. "Poe uses the word 'pentagon' multiple times here. When Rowena lies dying, the narrator describes a goblet and drops of blood. Later, after death, the body reanimates as Ligeia. Poe has created something *occult*."

I sketched a star inside of the shape. "If I add this, the setting of the chamber suggests something important. What?"

"It's a pentagram, right? Like, devil worshiping and stuff?" one of my students, Kara, responded. She looked a little goth with her dyed black hair and heavy eyeliner, so I wasn't surprised she had some knowledge. "Was the narrator summoning the devil to transfer the soul or something?"

"I'm not an expert on the occult," I said, "but I *do* know that this symbol can be religious rather than satanic unless it's inverted. A pentagram is sometimes the star itself, or sometimes there's a star within one or two circles."

I added all to the board. "There's a controversy over whether the one in the circle is a pentagram versus a pentacle, and whether they're two different things or not, but most people agree that these symbols are powerful."

My relation was a bit of a stretch and one I wouldn't have gotten into under normal circumstances, but I doubted that students would think the digression was too far out. I cared about their learning, but today's lesson was more for me to show the person who might be watching—or listening, whatever way they were keeping tabs on me—that I knew about the witchcraft connection.

It had been only two weeks since we learned of Hadley's death, yet the different parts of the semester seemed cleaved as with a hatchet. As my students left the classroom, many continuing the animated discussions they had started, I gathered up my belongings, not pausing to erase the symbols I had drawn on the board.

Let them be seen.

---

No one showed up for office hours, and I managed to stay focused during that time and actually get some papers graded. My job was on the line—Candace had hinted that there might be a chance for another tenure-track position opening up in the department as long as one of the current faculty went through with his planned retirement, so I needed to do well. I had set my bait, and I would bide my time until something else happened. I still had a career to remake.

As it turned out, I didn't have to wait long.

---

Yawning as I reached my apartment complex, having suffered frequent restless nights since the announcement of Hadley's death, I made a mental checklist of my dinner options, all of which were frozen.

I stopped in the foyer to check my mail, thankful for the locked boxes. Nothing special—bills and junk. I didn't get much personal mail any longer, having shut most of my friends out of my life following Emma's death. No wedding invitations, baby showers, or reunions anymore.

I needed to exert more effort at reestablishing friendships. Whatever was going on with Jake, who had dutifully called during my lunch but had little time to talk, that was something else. I missed having close female friends.

A wave of exhaustion hit me as I approached my apartment door. I wanted jammies and a little time on the couch to eat my Lean Cuisine, and then I'd go to bed. I held up my key, ready to stick it in the lock.

There was no need. My apartment door was already cracked open.

## Chapter 27

There was no way I left that morning without closing the door. No possible way. I had a choice: either call 911 and report a break-in, or see for myself what had been done.

I wasn't expecting the news of my little pentagram/pentacle lesson to have spread so fast. Maybe one of the Poppies *was* in my class, after all.

With a lump in my throat, adrenaline coursing through my bloodstream, I opened the door wide.

"I'm home. Is someone here?"

I was hit with a horrible thought. *Where was Norman?* The door was open, and he could have gotten out. Or worse. Someone may have wanted to send a message.

"Norman?"

Nothing. Then again, he didn't always come when called. He was a cat, not a dog. I opened the pantry and grabbed his jar of treats, shaking it to get his attention, trying to stop the bad thoughts from overtaking me.

"Norman! Where are you?" I darted my eyes around the apartment, looking for Norman but also taking in the details of my surroundings, any trace of movement or object out of place.

My right eye started twitching. I wanted to find him more than anything, yet I was also terrified of what I might discover.

Maybe I *should* have "stopped." Norman was my constant companion for years. I knew I'd lose him someday, but if I had invited harm on him—I shuddered to think of it.

*Think. Be logical*, I told myself. Norman had a habit of finding hiding places wherever we'd lived, especially if it was time to trim his nails, give him his flea treatment, or take him to the vet. He could be *fine*.

I glanced into my office, half expecting to see the room tossed like in the movies, the desk drawers torn out and papers ripped up and covering the floor. Everything looked just as I left it.

"Norman!" If I called enough, maybe he'd hear the worry in my voice and come out. I was no animal psychologist, but I knew from my history with cats that they sometimes intuited when their owners were sad.

I opened up my bedroom closet, just in case he had run inside without me knowing it in the morning, but all I saw were clothes and shoes. It was a two-bedroom apartment— there weren't that many places to search. There was a real possibility that he was missing, that he sneaked out the door or was taken as a further warning.

Sitting down at the kitchen table, I could no longer keep the guilt at bay. *I* had done this. My cat was gone, and it was all because I decided to push the buttons of a person or people who were dangerous, people who had left a girl dead in the woods.

The irony was not lost on me.

Then I heard it—a tiny meow, muffled. He was here, somewhere in the apartment.

Running around like a maniac, I looked under the couch,

threw open the kitchen cabinet doors, and found him in the hall closet with my jackets, boots, and umbrellas.

"What are you doing in here, sweetie?" I picked him up, holding his black, furry body close to mine until he scrambled to get away. Like me, he wasn't really a hugger.

Was it all in my head? I had used this closet that morning when getting my coat, and I'd been so distracted that I could have stupidly not checked the door. Maybe no one was after me. Jake could be right—I was probably paranoid. If someone was trying to warn me off, they were certainly being passive about it.

After giving Norman his late dinner and a bunch of extra treats, plus one more round of cuddling on his terms, I tried to shrug off the day. My stomach growled from hunger, but I forced myself to wash my face and change into my pajamas first so I could relax and then have an easier transition to bed. Finally, I opened the freezer to grab my food.

That's where I saw it, where I might not have looked if I had chosen to pick up takeout or cook something. It was as if whoever put it there knew my routine on a Monday night, home late and a microwaved dinner.

Another note, this one with a pentacle drawn on it.

# CHAPTER 28

## THEN

As the Jeep pulled up to the darkened sorority house, Marissa realized that it was yet another object that had lost its luster. When she started pledging, she viewed this singular location as a symbol of belonging; if she could endure and earn her OKB letters, she would feel that she had made it. If things were different, she might have moved into this house of hedonism after some older sisters graduated. Marissa had expected to transition into one of the girls of OKB, throwing parties, walking around in a jacket that showed exactly who she was: a sister. Someone who mattered, part of the in-crowd.

Now, looking through eyes that had metamorphosed and dulled in the last few hours, she perceived it for what it was, a crumbling rowhouse shared by a group of girls whose biggest commonalities were drinking and hooking up with random guys. What did sisterhood even mean at this point, when Kai, her closest friend, was alone in the woods, never to return?

Phoebe unlocked the door with her house key and held a finger to her lips. "Don't talk about it. We protect ourselves if we don't even *think* about it. Kai left during the night, and you don't know where she went. Get some sleep. You only have a few hours. I'll take care of the clothes, and then I'll get some sleep, too."

The girls slipped into the house and crept down the basement stairs, fearful of each creak.

*No one else can know.* The eight girls had entered a sisterhood of secrets, one to which none of them wished to belong.

Settling onto the floor, overcome with mental and physical exhaustion, the girls tried to sleep. Marissa heard someone—she wasn't sure whom—whispering in the dark, but Hannah's unmistakable alto voice rang through the night: "We're not gonna talk about it. Go to sleep."

Marissa closed her eyes and prayed for forgiveness. From God, if He existed. More importantly, from Kai, her true, brave friend whom she had abandoned and covered up like an animal. She felt the hot tears leak out of her eyes as she tried to follow Phoebe's directions: *Don't think about it.*

She summoned the image of a rug in her mind and visualized sweeping everything under it. But no matter how hard she tried, she couldn't get the picture out of her head: Kai in the makeshift grave, her flesh soon to rot from her bones.

———

MARISSA ROUSED to a heavy clanging and the same discombobulation she had experienced all week when awakening on this hard floor, feeling the crick in her neck and discomfort in her back and legs. Irritated by the noise and groggy from lack of sleep, she needed a few moments to remember. But then the events of the previous night ambushed her, sending her back into a fear-stricken state.

Danielle stood over her, banging together a pot and pan. "Good morning, pledges! Wakey, wakey!" She had a huge grin on her face, oblivious to the midnight outing.

Marissa fully opened her eyes, taking in the sisters standing around her, some yawning and looking hungover, others bright-eyed like they could go for a brisk run. Courtney, Angela, and Phoebe hung together, their faces mirroring the same bleak expression Marissa imagined graced her own countenance.

Courtney stepped forward. "Pledges, your Big Sisters will blindfold you and lead you upstairs. We ask you to trust us this morning, just as we have asked you to put your faith in us these last several weeks." Marissa thought she heard Courtney's voice waver.

Phoebe came up behind her with a folded-up bandana and squeezed her hand. For solidarity? In warning? Marissa didn't know, but she could feel Phoebe's flesh tremble on top of her own.

"Guys?" Maribeth broke the silence. "Where's Kai? She's not here. Where'd she go?"

In the crowded basement of pledges and sisters, Kai's absence hadn't been noticed until this moment as her Big Sister searched for her. Marissa tried to fashion an expression of surprise as she pretended to look around the room.

"Did she sneak upstairs to use the bathroom?" someone asked.

"I'll check," Maribeth said, running up the stairs. The girls waited, some of them knowing that Kai would *never* return to that basement, others assuming Kai might be worried about getting in trouble for missing the start of the function. They waited, hearing the slap of feet on the floorboards overhead.

Maribeth thundered down the stairs a couple of minutes later. "She's not there." Her heart-shaped face held a real look of concern; Marissa knew that Maribeth had been kind to Kai during pledging, helping her figure out time management and giving her little treats and gifts. "Does anyone have any idea where she is? I remember her being here last night. We talked. She was definitely here."

"She was sleeping right next to me," Jessica said, the lie rolling off her tongue. *Was* it a lie? Kai *did* sleep there—briefly, before they all went to the woods.

"She wouldn't just leave, would she? We didn't even have a crazy function last night. Why would she leave?" Danielle's voice carried a note of panic. As the president of OKB, she could potentially have trouble to deal with if a pledge shared any secrets of the organization. "Did she take her stuff? I can't imagine she'd have left in her hell clothes. It was *freezing* last night. She'd catch a cold."

Hannah pointed to the wall. "She didn't take her backpack. It's right here."

"As the president of this sorority, I don't want to disrespect Kai's privacy, but I'm honestly freaking out a little right now. Can someone please check her bag and see if her street clothes, wallet, and keys are in there?"

Marissa stepped forward, her blood pumping in her ears. *Should they have gotten rid of Kai's bag, too, to make it look like she had decided to leave?* She thought back to Phoebe's orders, how they all needed to maintain that Kai had left on her own, that the function in the woods had never occurred. "I'll check."

She thought about lying, about concealing what she found, but she couldn't get away with that in front of everyone. Marissa unzipped the main compartment of the backpack and pulled out the sweater and jeans Kai had worn to class over her hell clothes just yesterday. She saw the biology textbook, Kai's pledge book, and a binder. Opening the smaller section, Marissa held up Kai's keys and wallet, articles Kai would never need again. "It's all here. She left *everything*."

"This doesn't make any sense," Maribeth said, sidling up to Marissa and looking into the backpack. "If she got pissed off and left, she would've taken her stuff with her. And why would she have gotten mad? We had fun last night, right? It was a fun function! She looked tired, but not like she was bursting to get out of here. I don't think she seemed upset."

"Well, she's not here, and I don't think aliens abducted her, so she's gotta be somewhere," Charity said, her face scrunched up into an annoyed expression. "I think we should just get on with things and see if she shows up later. Maybe she had plans for some guy to pick her up here. Does anyone know if she was seeing anyone? I don't know when she'd have the time, but maybe she arranged to sneak out and meet him and had no idea we'd be up so early looking for her. Maybe she's asleep in some dude's comfy bed right now instead of in the basement with the rest of us schmucks."

"In her hell clothes, filthy? You think she'd arrange to meet someone all disgusting like that? I think she'd be humiliated," Maribeth challenged. "Was she super drunk? She didn't seem that drunk when we were talking. Tipsy, maybe. Geez, I hope she's okay."

Marissa looked down at her own appearance. Her hair, even held back in a ponytail, was a rat's nest, her clothes caked in baby powder and worse, grime and beer from the basement floor. She could smell herself, stale sweat and body odor. She noticed the dirt under her fingernails—dirt from last night, from helping clear the hollow area under the tree—and curled her fingers inward, hiding them. No, it was hard to believe Kai would've walked out here for a hookup. And then it came to her.

"I wonder if she was sleepwalking," she said, remembering the Ritual of Secrets from the other night, feeling guilty for saying something she knew to be both private and, in this case, completely untrue.

Jessica's eyes brightened. "Oh my God, I bet you're right! She said it was a problem when she was little, and it was really embarrassing since she was at her friend's house for a sleepover one time and sleepwalked into the older brother's room. He woke up and she was curled up on the floor."

Kai had been mortified, of course, and had thought this to be one of the most uncomfortable moments of her life, but some of her pledge sisters had struggled not to laugh, especially after the other far more serious revelations.

Marissa smiled for a moment at her cleverness in finding a solution to the puzzle but quickly rearranged her expression into one of concern, tamping down the bitter truth that was so much darker than a sleepwalking episode.

"Should we go look for her? I don't know how sleepwalking works, but she could be in danger. Should we call the cops?" Maribeth suggested.

"I wouldn't want her to get in trouble for underage drinking if they pick her up and she smells like booze. Maybe she *just* left. Maybe she woke up early and needed a walk and wasn't thinking. I think we should just go ahead with the plan for now," Phoebe said, her voice steady. "Sleepwalking is just one theory. All we know for sure is that she's not here, and we can go look around later. Maybe she walked back to her dorm and asked the RA to let her in."

"If she showed up in her hell clothes and went to the RA, there's a good chance we're getting a call from administration later," Charity said. "I hope she wouldn't be that much of a dumbass to do that."

"Our RA's just a sophomore, too. No way she'd report us. *If* that's even what happened. I know Kai wouldn't want anybody to get in trouble, no matter where she is." Jessica sounded so convincing that Marissa began picturing these other realities, alternate versions of the truth where Kai was somehow safe and sound.

"Okay. That settles it. Let's focus on the ceremony for now and figure out the Kai situation later," Danielle said, terminating the discussion. "All right. Big Sisters, please place the blindfolds on your Little Sisters' eyes and lead them up the stairs."

Phoebe tied the bandana taut on Marissa's head. "Nice work," she whispered, so soft that Marissa couldn't be certain if Phoebe was saying these words or if it was her own internal voice. "We can do this. Stick to the plan."

She walked upstairs, holding the banister, feeling nauseated for the lies she had told but worse for what she knew to be the truth.

"Okay, Big Sisters, remove the blindfolds," Courtney said.

Marissa opened her eyes to red and black balloons filling the room. A cake and several bottles of champagne graced the table.

"Congratulations, girls, you're sisters now!" Angela said, the enthusiasm in her voice coming out insincere. She busied herself by cutting and handing out pieces of the cake, slicing right through the large OKB letters.

Marissa tried to smile. This was what she had wanted for so long. She felt something and saw that Phoebe had placed a sorority jacket around her shoulders, the silky, smooth black fabric giving off warmth which she had sought since before last night's outing.

"Have a glass of champagne, eat some cake, and enjoy! Go home and take a shower afterward—God knows you all need them. Then come back tonight for a proper celebration. We're getting a keg and inviting Sig Ep over for a mixer. You've done it, ladies! Cheers!" Danielle announced as she filled red plastic cups.

The sickening sweetness of the cream cheese icing stuck in her throat, so Marissa downed a large gulp of the cheap champagne.

Later, back in her dorm, she took a long, hot shower, lathering herself up with body wash on her loofah. But as hard as she scrubbed, as red and raw as she scoured her skin, she couldn't seem to remove the feeling of dirtiness, no matter how much filth swirled down the drain.

She sat down on her bed and waited for a knock on the door or for the phone to ring. She waited to be caught.

# CHAPTER 29

No one ever found Kai. I kept waiting, either for someone to discover her body or for one of the other girls to tell, but it never happened.

The morning after we were initiated into the sorority, when no one had heard from Kai, Danielle decided we needed to call the cops. The whole group of us agreed to leave out the part about sleeping in the basement and wearing hell clothes—those parts were changed to "having a sleepover" and "wearing only her pajamas"—but we sat down in the living room with an officer who took notes. He seemed dismissive at first, coming to the same innocuous conclusions as some of the sisters, but the next several days, with no sign of Kai, put the case into overdrive.

I remember being called in for a formal witness statement. They took me into an interrogation room and asked me to describe my friend to them, what she was like and where I thought she had gone. Though I shook my head and lied that I had no idea, the tears that streamed from my eyes were real enough.

Kai's parents asked to speak with me, and I told them the

same thing. I didn't know what happened to her, but I missed her very, very much. At least the latter part was true.

It was as if I sleepwalked through the rest of the semester, going to my classes and attending parties, carrying the secret around like a boulder inside my chest. I couldn't help but look at Kai's empty desk during biology.

Kai's disappearance had cast a pall not just over my sorority but all of campus, with everyone harboring their own thoughts on what had happened to her, some spinning wild theories. A number of students withdrew from Blackthorn since they worried that it was unsafe, that they could be the next to disappear without a trace.

Maribeth talked about Kai the most. After all, she had no idea what really happened, but those of us who knew didn't speak of her, didn't want to put the grisly horror into words.

"I think I see her at night sometimes in my room," Jessica confided after too many mixed drinks at a party one night. "I know she's not there. But I look at her empty bed and feel like she is." I didn't say anything, and we never spoke of it again.

Somehow, I made it through to Christmas break and looked forward, for once, to going home, back to the trailer park. I shut myself in my shared room with Annie, who was brimming with excitement to hear about my sorority and college life in general.

My sister told me she was disappointed that my weekly letters to her had trailed off, but I shut her up by explaining that my best friend had disappeared, and Annie gave me the space I needed. I never told my parents what happened, but they barely interacted with me other than my mom muttering some comments about me being stuck up for pledging a sorority.

I focused on pushing down that image of Kai's body, which came to me unbidden when I least expected it, sometimes just from the crunch of a leaf underfoot. I struggled to keep it at bay, filling my brain with something else, like going through the different state capitals, when the darkness seeped through. Over time, it became easier not thinking about it.

When the new semester started, I skipped the first sorority meeting. I tried to attend; I walked all the way to the sorority house, but I couldn't force myself to go inside—I felt too raw. Later that week, I turned in my letter jacket and apologized. Danielle surprised me with a hug. "I understand. Everything changed with Kai."

It turns out I wasn't the only one. Hannah didn't return to Blackthorn; she dropped out, I learned. Janelle turned in her letter jacket, as well. Of our pledge class, only Jessica remained active in the sorority.

When I bumped into any of the sisters on campus, we'd wave but not engage. No hard feelings, apparently; I wouldn't be one of the cautionary tales for future pledge classes to memorize. I heard that OKB didn't participate in rush in the spring, or maybe they did, but no one decided to pledge. Whatever happened, I stopped seeing OKB jackets by my senior year of college, or maybe I stopped searching for them.

I refocused myself on my studies. My GPA had slipped a bit during the semester I pledged, so my scholarship was in jeopardy. It gave me every justification to leave my sorority days in the past and focus on my future. I asked for more hours at the library and loaded up on credits, adding a creative writing minor to complement my English literature major.

I tried to bury my association with Omega Kappa Beta just as we'd buried Kai. And I almost succeeded.

---

THE PIECE of paper in the freezer brought all those memories rushing back. There was no question this time. The note's meaning was unmistakable: "I know about Kai and am ready to tell. You need to stop looking into Hadley's death."

Those words, combined with the pentacle, let me know that the threat was real, not imagined. They had heard about my little stunt in class today and had revved up their own game.

I let out the sigh I'd been holding inside. Here it was, blatant in Times New Roman font. If I showed the note to Jake, he couldn't fob it off as anything but a menace to my safety, but that would mean I'd have to come clean about my own buried secret—my very *criminal* secret. The stakes were clear: If I kept trying to help solve Hadley's murder, my own sins would be spilled for all the world to see.

But why? What the hell did the Poppies—if that's who wrote this, if that's who was threatening me—have to do with Kai? How did they *know*? For all these years, I'd been holding my breath, waiting to get called back in for questioning, expecting some Boy Scout or hiker at Water's Edge to discover Kai's body and have the police batter down my door since my DNA would probably be found on it. We had left Kai in that hole twenty-four years ago, and my seven co-conspirators and I had always put ourselves first.

I had made a terrible choice back then and carried an albatross around my neck ever since. Now, I had to choose again. If I kept digging, maybe I could help Hadley's parents find closure, yet I'd jeopardize my future.

Things with Jake were so new. He had let his guard down for me, no easy feat, and here I was hiding something sure to damage our tenuous bond. How could he, a man of the law, be with *me*, a criminal? It didn't matter that I had lived my life on the straight and narrow except for that single incident. My decision to go along with covering up Kai's death changed who I was. Could I claim to be a good person after that? Did I even *deserve* happiness?

And then there was my career. I *might* get off with a fine and a misdemeanor—I had googled variations of "hiding an accidental death" and "concealing a body" scores of times from public computers over the years so the search history couldn't be found on my personal laptop, and those were two of the lighter punishments. "Abuse of a corpse" was a felony, though, and the statute of limitations wouldn't have run out even after all this time.

Whatever charge I received, I imagined it wouldn't bode well for future employment, not at Blackthorn University, where I'd lied all those years ago, and not anywhere else. And it could be worse: jail time of up to a year in Pennsylvania, not as much as in some other states. As far as I could figure out without actually contacting a lawyer, additional charges could include lying to police and tampering with evidence, both of which incurred penalties.

And I wasn't the only person whose life could fall apart; there were the other girls to worry about, as well—women, now, all of us in our early-to-mid forties. I wasn't in touch with anyone from the past, wishing to forget them and the horrible thing we had done, just as I'm sure they wanted to forget me. I'd ignored the Facebook friend request I'd received from Phoebe about ten years ago, not wanting to dredge up the past, and deleted, unread, the Messenger post she'd sent a few years after that. Whatever she had to say, I preferred not to hear. Luckily, she was the only one who had reached out.

I had searched the internet for all of them over the years, even setting up Google alerts, each of those other seven girls who had been on the cliff that night and left Kai alone in the animal's den. It's amazing what you can find even without police resources, and I wanted to keep track. Janelle had died in a car crash a few years after I graduated. The internet was pretty new back then, and I didn't find many details. While I felt for her, the evil part of me breathed a sigh of relief: only six girls remained who could tear apart my life. And Hannah overdosed about ten years ago. The obit I saw only mentioned that she passed, but a deep dive on Facebook revealed to me that she had relapsed.

That meant I was down to five: Jessica, a first-grade teacher who was married with two kids; Abby, who worked in finance and was a lacrosse coach at a local high school; Courtney, a stay-at-home mom who homeschooled her four children; Phoebe, a real estate lawyer; and Angela, who was alive as far as I could tell, but I couldn't find out anything else about her career or family. I discovered a court case about her suing her landlord, but that was it.

I located material on my former sisters on MySpace (back in the day), Facebook, Instagram, LinkedIn, Twitter, local online newspapers, and more. During my marriage, I crept downstairs in the middle of the night when I couldn't sleep and searched for any shred of information I could find about my co-conspirators. When I was going through IVF, and later, when pregnant, amped up on hormones, my late-night searches became even more manic. I couldn't help but wonder if my involvement in the coverup of Kai's death had cursed me.

We each managed to move on in some way, finding a life. We all left Kai to decay in that shallow grave while we reinvented ourselves as responsible humans. And we were all liars. I felt it every day, even when I tried to keep those thoughts in the recesses of my brain.

I also searched for Kai's family in my darkest times. All these years later, they still had hope that she'd return. Someone had started a GoFundMe at some point, and I'd donated anonymously from a computer at a library with a credit card I opened and closed to use that once.

As much as I hungered for material about them, it was agonizing seeing their plight: all those pictures of Kai, frozen in time at nineteen. I speculated on how she'd look now, if she had lived, if I'd be able to see the gray in her blonde hair the way mine could be seen in my brown. I wondered if she'd have a crease in her forehead like I had, the one that David told me was "really starting to show my age" back before I even turned forty.

How I missed her, my one true friend.

But, if anyone cracked, if anyone shared what happened that night, *all* of our lives could come crashing down. Since the police had never knocked on my door about Kai's death, I assumed that no one had talked, that they'd all kept the dirty secret as I had.

With this note, though, it meant that someone *had* told. Not the cops, but they told *some*one, most likely the person who left the note. How did one of my former sorority sisters connect to this person? Did this mean that the deaths were somehow linked? That didn't make any sense.

Two dead girls, both Blackthorn University students, separated by almost twenty-five years. Their bodies had both been *in* Water's Edge, even if Hadley's corpse had been found and Kai's hadn't. What else did they have in common? They both were pledging sororities. And they both were connected to *me*. A chill passed through me as I realized the extent of the similarities.

I could do what Jake instructed me and turn my back on Hadley's case. That didn't mean her murder had to remain unsolved—Jake and his partner were professionals who had cleared other homicides. If I went back to worrying about my teaching and scholarship, I'd be safe from the murderer or murderers.

Or, I could keep digging and take my chances. If the Poppies were responsible for the note, they were probably involved in Hadley's death, too. I didn't want to underestimate them, but they were young and bound to make some mistakes. They weren't the *Mafia*; they didn't have unlimited resources and hitmen or anything crazy like that.

Maybe Hadley's death was an accident, just like Kai's, and the girls were scared, as we had been, thinking of self-preservation more than anything else. That didn't account for the roofies found in Hadley's system, but maybe it was part of their pledging. My pledge sisters and I were forced to drink alcohol, and maybe Hadley's pledge class was required—or at least coerced—to take drugs.

I could see it happening. I'd researched pledging rituals over the years, and some were innocuous while others were deadly. It all went back to the bizarre traditions that organizations honored. If only we hadn't gone to the cliff that night for that stupid ritual, maybe Kai and I would chat once a month and get together every couple of years or so.

But we *did* go to that cliff, and Kai fell. And we all decided to cover up her death.

There was another option. I didn't really want to consider it, but it was time, after all these years. I had avoided it for this long.

# CHAPTER 30

It was after ten p.m., but I called anyway, expecting to leave a message since most people avoid picking up when it's an unknown number. I'd planned what to say in advance so that I didn't give too much away but would entice her to call me back.

"Hello?"

"Hi. It's Marissa Owens, from college. From OKB. I'm sorry to call you so late, but I think we need to talk."

Phoebe paused. I expected she was as surprised to hear from me as I was in making this call. "Little Sister. I wondered if I'd ever hear from you again. I reached out to you a couple times." She sounded tired, her words hollow, emotionless.

"I don't want to say too much over the phone, but it's about college. Someone told me they have information regarding that situation. Someone knows."

As ashamed as I was to reduce Kai's tragic death to a "situation," I needed to code my words. Anyone could be listening. Someone had broken into my apartment and hidden my cat to get a rise out of me. I had no doubt that things could escalate.

"You're sure? You are really, truly sure that this 'someone' knows? Why now, after all these years?" Phoebe demanded, bringing me back to all those times she'd made requests of me during pledging.

"It's complicated, and I can tell you more in person, but I think we need to meet. I'm more comfortable if we can talk face-to-face."

Phoebe sighed. "We had a deal, all of us. We weren't *ever* supposed to talk about it, not with anyone else and not even with each other."

"Well, *someone* broke that deal. I haven't talked to anyone else. Two of us aren't even alive anymore, and I doubt that one of them told, since they've been gone for years and it's only coming up now."

"Why me? Why did you call *me*? I have a lot to cope with as it is," Phoebe said. "Why not one of the others?"

"Because, Phoebe," I explained, "it was *your* idea not to go for help. I think you may have the most to lose. I want to meet and talk it over. I can't talk to anybody else about this. I have a life, too, and I don't want to deal with this, but if *we* don't, someone else might. I think you once told me to be proactive rather than reactive, didn't you?"

Phoebe stayed quiet for nearly a minute, and I wondered what she was doing, whether she was looking up information or texting anyone. For all I knew, she could still be in touch with one or more of the other girls.

"Yes. We should talk, and we can figure out where to go from here. You need to tell me *everything* about what this person knows, what they said. I can meet tomorrow at seven o'clock or later; I need time to travel. Can we meet at the site? I don't know where you're located. Is that doable? It'll be dark, and we shouldn't have any company by then." Casual, like we were meeting for a Craigslist sale.

"I can do that. Seven o'clock at the site, the bottom, not

the top." Technically, there were two places: the cliff and the grave.

"Okay. See you then," she responded, all business. No goodbye, for we were far removed from two friends catching up. No, we were two criminals figuring out whether or not our dirty deed would finally come to light.

I was sick of the evasions, the fibs and outright lies. Telling the secret could allow the release of some of the darkness I carried. But, before I made any moves, I felt that I needed to talk to someone else who had been there, someone else whose life could be royally jacked up from their role in the coverup. Besides, Phoebe was an actual lawyer now, not just a pre-law student. Even though her specialty was real estate law, she probably had some background in criminal defense and knew lawyers who could help us. On the face of it, for all her ruth-lessness, she could be the best person out of the group for me to talk to.

Or the worst.

# CHAPTER 31

T he next day, I walked around in a fog, completing tasks by muscle memory: taking care of the cat, watering houseplants, running. Tuesday was my lightest workday of the week, so only a limited number of students were exposed to my distraction. I wasn't on my game; I needed to get it together at work, or my evaluations might be so bad that I wouldn't have a shot at continuing at Blackthorn after my one-year contract was up.

Then again, depending on the outcome of the meeting with Phoebe, my entire career trajectory was uncertain, as was my freedom.

Jake was waiting for me outside my office after class, not even sitting on the couch but standing at my door, a Starbucks coffee in each hand. He must have memorized my schedule as well as my routine—I always came back to my office to retrieve my purse and laptop before heading home.

"Venti skinny vanilla latte, right? Do you have a minute?"

"Hi. I wasn't expecting to see you." As I unlocked my office door, I glanced sideways, trying to read his face.

"I was on campus looking into something and thought I'd

drop by." He sat down in one of my office chairs and sipped his coffee. "Not enough sugar." He ripped open a packet, dumped it in, and swirled it around.

"No Welch today?" I swallowed a mouthful of coffee and tried to look nonchalant, not wanting to give up any clues of my distress over my upcoming meeting with Phoebe.

"He's off exploring another angle. Besides, I figured I'd come say hi since I was already here." He touched my arm and smiled.

"Good timing. I just finished my class and was about to head home to grade papers. I'm meeting a friend later, someone from college." The half-lie rolled off my tongue. My pulse started racing, more from nerves than the touch. *Was he here as my lover, or as a cop?*

"Oh." I couldn't tell if it was disappointment in his voice, but we hadn't made plans, and it was way too early for him to think we'd spend every night together.

"A woman," I clarified. "Someone from my old sorority." *Stop talking. He doesn't need to know.*

"You know, Marissa, speaking of your sorority, I was wondering about something," he started, unceremonious, like we were just two people who wanted to learn more about each other. "The girl who disappeared when you were in college. Kai. Your friend. Is there any way that witchcraft might have been involved back then? I was thinking what a coincidence it was, two girls disappearing while pledging a sorority at Blackthorn, both of them connected to you."

So I wasn't the only one who noticed. "I wasn't in the *Poppies*, Jake. OKB practiced the art of beer pong, not witchcraft." I took a long sip to bide my time. "And you've seen every *inch* of me. I don't have any pentacle tattoos. Other than my black cat, there's nothing witchy about me."

"I had to ask. In my job, we don't like a coincidence." His dark eyes bore into mine.

I sighed. "I'm connected with a number of tragedies. Missing friend. Dead mom. Dead baby. Dead marriage. Now dead student. Are these all coincidences? Should I dig deeper into all of my baggage?"

He reached out, placing his hand in my upturned palm, which I noticed was tremoring with an emotion I couldn't quite place. "Hey, I didn't mean to upset you."

I let it stay there a moment before I clasped back. But all I needed was for a student or colleague to walk by and see me holding hands with the detective investigating Hadley's death for rumors to start flying. I wasn't even ready to tell Candace about this, whatever *this* was, and I'd known her forever.

I pulled my hand back, but I smiled at him. "No, it's fine. I get that you're doing your job."

"Actually, I was thinking about *your* job, too. About Poe. I'm not a huge reader, not like you, but I enjoy some crime fiction here and there. You know, Dennis Lehane, Richard Price, Michael Connelly, writers like that. I thought, 'Why not read something from the father of the detective story?'"

A smile touched the corners of my lips. "You knew that Poe invented detective stories?"

"I didn't know, not until you told me. So I read 'The Purloined Letter.'"

I grimaced. "That's my least favorite of the three. I would've recommended 'Murders in the Rue Morgue.'"

"Not gonna lie, I wasn't blown away. Too talky. But something *did* stick with me, Marissa. You know how the guy, the head police prefect or whatever, has his team search the minister's entire house for the missing letter, even peering inside the legs of tables and chairs? They were so thorough. But they didn't *find* the letter that way. They looked in all kinds of good hiding places, but it was in plain sight, in the most obvious place, with his other letters."

He paused a beat, maybe waiting for me to give him a gold

star for his summary, maybe wondering if he could make me sweat. "I've been acting like those French police, looking in all the nooks and crannies, when I need to be more like Dupin—however you pronounce his name. There's something obvious that I'm missing. It's like it's on the tip of my tongue, but I haven't quite gotten inside the suspect's head. Not yet."

I refused to bite. "I can't pretend to understand the intricacies of an investigation, Jake, but I'm sure you'll figure it out." *Let him stick to Hadley for now and not think too much about coincidences or obvious places*, I hoped.

"You're a fascinating woman, Marissa Owens," Jake said. "But I need to get back to work. And I know you have those papers to grade."

Later, after he left me to think about everything, what he said and left unsaid, I couldn't help but go through the *what-ifs*.

*What if* Kai and I hadn't pledged? *What if* she hadn't fallen that night? *What if* we had gone to the cops right away and dealt with whatever punishment we would have received?

Through my research of similar cases, I learned a sobering truth: If we had called the authorities, the other pledges and I probably wouldn't have gotten in trouble for anything more than underage drinking, if that. If we had called the police, *maybe* everything would have been okay. I had read numerous articles where accidental deaths that occurred during hazing resulted in relatively minor consequences.

The sisters would have received some punishment for hazing, probably, but it was the late nineties, and most of the hazing laws weren't in effect yet. They might have received, at most, a week in jail, maybe community service, expulsion from college, and/or a mark on their records. If I had just followed my gut that night and done the right thing, I wouldn't have had to deal with twenty-four years of dread.

But, when we moved Kai's body, changed her into

Angela's clothes, hid her, and lied to the police, we escalated things from a tragic accident to an actual crime with the possibility of multiple charges. My stomach roiled as I contemplated how that single night, with that terrible decision to go along with the lie, shrouded the rest of my life. All the good deeds I had done, every selfless or kind act, paled in comparison to my choice on Hell Night.

I could no longer hide. It was time to come clean, but I needed to talk it through with Phoebe first. I wasn't ready to go to the authorities, especially one handsome detective in particular whose response might make me feel worse than I already did.

---

THE BLACKENED trees reached out across the road to join their limbs, giving the impression of a tunnel, or maybe a portal to my past. I drove in silence, knowing I needed the brain space to think. While my soul yearned for soothing, it seemed inappropriate to enjoy music as I prepared for the conversation with my Big Sister.

Even while driving, I felt the weight of the switchblade in my jacket pocket, an unwelcome presence. I purchased it earlier that day with cash and some non-threatening supplies —a sleeping bag and camping lantern—at Walmart, hiding my intention in case anyone was watching.

I wasn't expecting that Phoebe would attack me, but I had to be ready; I didn't know to what lengths she'd be willing to go to protect our secret, but it was one of the reasons I wanted to meet at Kai's grave instead of at the cliff itself. Proximity to a cliff might be too tempting if Phoebe hoped to keep me quiet.

One thing looked fairly certain: Phoebe couldn't be the one who sent the note. Exposing my sins would unmask her own unless this was all a bluff and she was somehow connected to the Poppies and/or Hadley's death. That seemed like a longshot, but I couldn't be too careful. If the conversation turned ugly, my main plan was to run. I didn't want more blood on my hands, but I needed protection just in case.

As I pulled into the dark, empty parking lot at Water's Edge, I was counting on two things: one, that the trails would be deserted from hikers and police due to nightfall, and two, that I'd remember where to go.

The passage of time failed to dull the ghastly details etched into my brain. I'd never come back to this dreadful place, not during the rest of my college career and not since I'd returned to the area, no matter how many times Candace had asked me to join her for a weekend hike. While others raved about the waterfalls and scenic lakeside views, all I felt here was regret.

Finding the placard for Otter Creek Trail with the strong, steady beam of my flashlight, I turned right. The frigid air cut through my Sherpa-lined fall jacket, but I was much warmer than on my last trek through Water's Edge.

Scanning the woods, I failed to see or hear any sign of Phoebe. But I was early. I focused on the crackle of dry leaves and searched for landmarks, specifically the cliff.

I steered clear but used it for guidance—from the cliff to the clearing, from the clearing to the hollow. The grave. A glance at my watch confirmed that it was only 6:45, so I sat down to wait, right next to the tree that provided shade but no warmth to my old friend, beside the small boulder that served as her unmarked, makeshift tombstone.

Placing my hand on the cool, smooth surface, I imagined Kai reaching out from the other side. "I'm so sorry," I murmured, the same words I managed to speak to her family members when they showed up at my dorm asking if I had any idea what could have happened.

LOST IN THOUGHT, I didn't hear Phoebe approach until she had almost reached me; the low moan of the late October wind all but drowned out her soft tread.

She turned on her flashlight, illuminating her face *Blair Witch*-style, all cheekbones and planes. "You're looking pretty cozy down there."

I rose to my feet, brushing leaves and debris off my jeans. "Let's cut to the chase and not get into theatrics," I said.

It wasn't a friendly reunion; we were two people who once knew each other, and now we were two people who had a common problem. I didn't want to draw her attention by placing my hand into my pocket, but I touched the side of my jacket, pretending to remove a leaf, to feel the reassuring presence of the switchblade.

Phoebe switched off the flashlight, plummeting us into near darkness, and pushed out a snort of a laugh, one staccato syllable. "Marissa, you haven't changed. Cold and collected, not an ounce of fun in your body. It's the main reason I selected you as my Little Sister. The other girls were more about partying, but you always went after what you wanted. So, I'm asking you now: What do you want?"

I considered her question for a moment, having no grounds to trust her, this woman I hadn't seen in more than twenty years.

"I want to talk to you and see if you know anything, and hear what you think. One of us told someone else what happened here that night, and now they're using that against me. I had a student who died, whose body was found here, in these very woods, and I was helping look into what happened. I've gotten threatening notes, but I don't want to stop searching for the truth. I want Hadley's parents to find out their daughter's fate so they can have closure."

"Hadley Parker. I heard about her, but I didn't realize you were at Blackthorn or knew her. I've kept tabs on you here and there over the years, but not lately. So much time has passed that I don't think about it that often, not now. I don't stay up every night wondering when the police will knock down my door and arrest me. Not anymore." Phoebe sighed, then fumbled in her pockets, bringing out a cigarette and lighter. The bright orange tip lit up in the darkness, and I was soon engulfed in an unwelcome cloud of smoke. "I regret it, too. But I need to know: Are you worried that someone *else* will expose what happened, or are you thinking of doing it yourself? I need to be prepared either way."

"I'm thinking about going to the police about Kai, admitting my role, but not ratting out everyone else. It's time. It's way *past* time. Everything with Hadley has brought back that night for me, and I don't want to hold the secret anymore." I sidestepped her smoke and added extra distance in case she didn't like what she heard.

"Why did you agree to meet me *here*, of all places?" she asked. "If *you* had suggested it, I might not have shown up."

"I think I had to come here, where it all went down, to be ready to face it," I said. "It needed to be here, where we left her."

Phoebe paused. In the darkness, I watched her blow out smoke rings. At one point, I would've been impressed.

"Are you ready to give up your life, your career, just so Kai's bones can be relocated to a cemetery? That's all that will happen. They'll move whatever's left of her—which won't be much, not after all this time—from here to somewhere else. And the cops *will* find out who else was involved, even if you don't give anyone's names. They'll check records and track down the rest of your pledge class. They'll interview every remaining member of the sorority to find out which ones of us were there.

"Most of the girls didn't even know we came here that night, but anyone from the pledge class might crack and name names. If your mysterious note writer knew *you* were involved with Kai, they probably have *all* of our names. Maybe someone's waiting to expose *everyone*."

Phoebe took her final puff and ground the cigarette into the earth. I bent to retrieve it, not wanting her to litter, but she had already picked it up to place back in her pack once it cooled down. "Relax, Marissa. I have *some* scruples."

"I might call a lawyer first, before I confess. I'm in the middle of a semester and I don't know what will happen to my students if I need to leave before the semester's over." I couldn't say the words *go to jail*, but they hung in the air between us like Phoebe's cigarette smoke, ready to choke me. "I don't know how I can face my students, my colleagues, anyone after this. I might not be able to teach anymore, once it's all out there."

"Then you need to be sure, really, truly sure, that this is what you want," Phoebe said. "Coming forward won't bring her back. Not Kai, and not Hadley. But grant one favor for me: Give me a few days to figure things out for myself, okay? I think that's fair. After all, I gave you the courtesy of a meeting, and I didn't lure you out here to push you off a cliff or anything. I'm not standing in your way even if it comes back on me."

I thought of the knife in my pocket. I hadn't known what to expect, but her calm acceptance surprised me. "Okay, but I *am* coming clean," I said. "I need to."

# CHAPTER 32

I tossed and turned all night from dreams I couldn't remember, which was for the best, as all that stuck behind was the sense of impending doom. This was compounded by the two texts I received before finishing my first cup of coffee.

The first was from Jake: *Hope you're not avoiding me after I surprised you yesterday at work. I'd love to see you tonight, NOT for police questioning.*

I wanted that, too, but I wasn't sure if I'd be seeing him across from a dinner table, in bed, or in an interrogation room. Even though I'd kept my secret about Kai from him, from everyone, since we had met, everything had keyed up with the threatening note and my decision—not fully embraced yet— to tell.

Jake was bound to discuss the case in some way, and I had knowledge I wasn't ready to share: the threatening note. He might sense that something was off and that I was withholding information. In general, despite the falsehoods I had told about what happened to Kai, I was a terrible liar, and I hated doing it. There was too much to keep track of. The easiest thing would be to feign disinterest in continuing our romance to prevent future hurt for us both, but I didn't know that I could pull off a lie of that magnitude. I cared about Jake, a lot.

As I pondered my response, my phone buzzed with the second text, this time from Candace: *We need to catch up about some work issues. Are you free for a drink tonight at my place?*

Candace wasn't a detective, so I felt more comfortable lying to her. *I already made plans with a gentleman caller,* I responded, which was nearly the truth and still could be. I figured my reference to *The Glass Menagerie* might amuse her and allow her to give me some space. Ever since David and I broke up, she had hounded me to "get back out there."

I expected a fun GIF or meme, in line with our regular texting, so her response took me aback. *I really must insist,* she wrote. *We need to talk about your Poe class the other night. I thought it would be better than having an official meeting in my office.*

Ouch. Candace had never taken that tone with me, not even when I was her student instead of colleague. She wasn't acting as a friend wanting a chat; she was a department chair who needed to haul a wayward employee into line. She was likely trying to soften the blow by offering to discuss it over drinks, treating me as both a friend *and* department member, but I couldn't pretend it didn't sting, especially with the word "official."

All I could figure was that a student, probably an ultra-religious one, must have been offended by my pentagram/pentacle lesson and gone to tattle on me. My point had been to stir the pot and try to coerce Hadley's killer to make another move, and that had worked, as proven by the B and E at my apartment.

But my lesson plan *was* educationally sound. While Poe never used the word pentagram or pentacle in any of his works, numerous scholars have brought up the significance of the pentagonal shape of Rowena's chamber as well as the references in several stories to the occult. I'd explain it all to Candace as I had to my students. As chair, she had to follow up on student complaints, but she respected me as an educator and would understand.

*Okay, let me know when you want me to show up. I'm free after my class ends at 6:15,* I responded.

We settled on seven o'clock to give me time to get home, eat a quick dinner, and take care of the cat before heading to her place. One of the last things I wanted was to lose Candace's esteem.

At least this made it a little easier to blow off Jake. *I'd love to see you, too, but my department chair's making me meet her for a drink. I think there was a student complaint about me. She said she'd otherwise need to talk to me in an "official" capacity,* I texted him with a worried emoji. I didn't know if he was an emoji user, but I was.

I saw bubbles, and I waited for his response, but then they disappeared.

*Maybe you could stop over later, around 10:00?* I wrote before the smarter, more mature side of me could stop myself.

His response, a simple thumbs-up, confirmed there was a lighter side to Jake Ruiz: He *was* an emoji user.

At some point during the day, in between classes, office hours, the potentially awkward meeting with Candace, and a probable booty call with Jake, I needed to figure out my next moves regarding the note writer(s) and how I'd handle my confession.

---

No EPIPHANIES STRUCK me as I slogged through my day; my comp classes and office hours were a piece of cake in comparison to everything else going on in my life. I felt a bit on edge during my Poe class, wondering who the informant was, but I'd had some silly complaints about my teaching throughout my career: I gave too much homework for a 100-level class (even though it was the only mandatory writing class the student would take and was therefore extremely important to their future college success); I gave too much feedback on writing (you are *most* welcome for working so hard to provide comments that will help you grow and stretch as a writer); I didn't grade fairly (please check the syllabus that explains my grading process and come to office hours to work through your questions rather than going over my head, dammit); there were more.

I had learned long ago how impossible it was to provide students with what they needed while also giving them what they wanted. In this instance, even though I'd taken the symbology route for a non-academic reason, I had the rationale to explain why I did it.

As I glanced around my classroom, I wondered if anyone had it out for me and was using this as a method to get me in trouble. Students generally *seemed* nice, but I'd read some mean and personal handwritten comments in the evaluations that went far beyond criticizing my teaching style. Since these messages were anonymous and only went to me, unlike the bubble sheet ratings which were kept on file, no one, however inappropriate, could be chastised for what they said. Someone once even critiqued how I parted my *hair*. Teaching evaluations, at times, needed to be taken with a grain of salt.

Often, I could easily detect the haters, those who squinted at me during class with barely contained disdain. Sometimes, they even spilled their venom publicly, telling me they didn't need a writing class, that they were excellent writers and this class competed with space for classes they required for their major.

*Hmm... your essay sings a different story.* Why was it so terrible to learn to improve? But I was distracting myself, focusing on the minutiae to avoid the larger problems with which I needed to deal.

I thought we had a good vibe going in this class, even with —or maybe especially because of—losing Hadley. Just the other week, when we read "Annabel Lee," I thought this class was feeling close to each other as well as to me. I must have been wrong, but I knew better than to take it so personally.

Part of my struggle as an introvert in an extroverted job was how to juggle my need for personal space with the social approval I craved just as much. I wanted to connect with my students and support them while simultaneously worrying that they were judging me, which they were. As they smiled and nodded, turned in papers, and chatted amiably with me during office hours, some of them were writing scathing reviews on *Rate My Professor*.

The truth was that I couldn't trust anyone to have my back. Period. Not my students, not my friend/department chair Candace, not my family, and definitely not my brand-new lover, who was good and true but probably wouldn't be able to get past the terrible confession that strove to burst out of me at any time. I was alone, again, as always.

The person with whom I'd had the most honest conversation in years was Phoebe, someone I didn't even know that well.

*Smile and nod. Act smart. Show them your pedigree.* I taught a kick-ass lesson that evening on Poe's use of irony. Go figure. I hoped that the student who complained, whoever that was, had learned something that day.

---

As I GOT ready for my meeting with Candace, I couldn't help but reflect on our many years of acquaintance and friendship. As a shy, friendless-again student recovering from a

(CRIME) trauma, I admired the youngish English professor I met during my junior year of college. Even though I hadn't worked to my full potential in Candace's Brit Lit 2 class, she campaigned for me to graduate with an English Department award and helped me find scholarships for grad school. Without Candace, I probably wouldn't have continued my education.

Was Candace a mother figure? No, more like a big sister. Though my mother hadn't seemed to care much about my accomplishments, I *had* a mother, at least, until I was twenty-one, and she made sure that I was fed and clothed. I don't know how much I was loved or cherished, but others had a far worse upbringing than I did. All it took was a few years of office hours to teach me that indifference wasn't the worst parental offense.

I'd been a guest at Candace's Victorian house at the top of the hill multiple times since moving back to Blackthorn. She tricked me into an awkward dinner party with other English faculty once, but normally it was just the two of us. Perpetually single, Candace had never mentioned a boyfriend or girlfriend in all the years I had known her. Respecting her privacy in her personal matters, I never prodded.

Candace bought the house after receiving tenure. A stately structure with towers and turrets, it needed a lot of TLC to bring it back to its former glory. I had refused her invitations to return to Blackthorn after graduating college, wanting to keep the past behind me, but she'd sent plenty of pictures of the extensive and expensive restoration process. With fresh gray shingles, a cobalt roof, and bay windows, the house became a landmark in the historic area of Blackthorn. Candace and I had recently sat on rocking chairs on her refurbished wraparound porch and drunk a bottle of wine, looking out at the town of Blackthorn spread before us like a feast. I'd felt relaxed and at home here. But, on this evening, the feeling of shame, unwarranted for this minor offense, descended upon me.

With my finger primed to ring the doorbell, I almost dropped the chilled bottle of wine I was carrying when Candace swung open the door. "Here," I said, trying to subdue my nerves.

"Oh, you didn't have to bring anything," she responded, taking the bottle and gesturing me inside. "Chilean Sauvignon Blanc? Lovely. I went on a wine tour in the Casablanca Valley in Chile years ago. Take a seat in the living room while I pour us each a glass. Let's have a few sips before we start our conversation."

Sitting on the edge of Candace's lush couch, I wished it would swallow me whole. I couldn't get a good read on her mood; she sounded normal enough, referencing one of her many fabulous adventures, but her text that morning had emphasized the mandatory nature of this gathering.

Unable to get a glimpse of her expression as she located stemless glasses and poured our wine, I tried to distract myself by looking over the familiar surroundings: the built-in shelving abundant with picture frames, candles, and souvenirs from her travels; the textured, patterned walls of the hallway; the row of fresh herbs growing in various pots in her farm-house-style kitchen. Candace's house matched her personal aesthetic: well-preserved, eclectic, and elegant.

Candace served the wine with a plate of cheese and crackers. Sitting in the wingback chair next to me, she took a deep sip. "Oh, sorry, I forgot to say 'cheers,'" she said, seeming preoccupied. She rambled on for a few minutes about something inconsequential and dull that happened at the farmer's market where she purchased the cheese. Maybe she was dreading our talk as much as I was. Even though we had never been on the same hierarchical level, with her filling roles as my professor, mentor, and now department chair over the years, our conversations had never sparked such trepidation.

I took another swig, grateful to have splurged on the pricier bottle rather than my old standby, whatever was on sale. The citrusy, refreshing taste placed an instant salve on my anxiety. After setting the glass down, I looked at Candace and waited, not wanting to delay the inevitable any longer.

"Alright. I'll come out with it. A student came to my office pretty upset first thing yesterday morning. Whenever a student seeks an audience with me, as department chair, I need to hear them out even if it's something petty. The student, who shall remain nameless to protect against retaliation in instances like this, claimed that you discussed and drew satanic symbols on the board during class on Monday, and they felt both scared and offended since they are a 'practicing Christian.'

"Since Poe is the father of horror, I would expect that the students are regularly exposed to some gory imagery in the literature itself. The student's claim, however, was that there was no such symbol in the actual works you were reading and that you were taking a great leap. Naturally, I assured the student that you are an expert in Poe, and that if you claim there's a connection to satanic symbols, there is. I also encouraged them to speak with you if they wanted so you could better explain in private that you were analyzing the literature and not attempting to push your personal beliefs onto them." Candace stopped to take a noisy gulp of wine and stuff a Triscuit and a piece of brie in her mouth.

Candace's brusque manner made me think I was still in hot water even though everything she said seemed in opposition to this. A student complained, but Candace backed me up, so I wondered why she was being so short with me. "Do you want me to explain how it's connected? It's all legit. There are a number of references to the occult in Poe's works, and we were discussing the shape of a bedchamber in one story—"

She cut me off with a chopping hand movement. "That's not necessary. I don't need to know all the details. I was not thrilled, however, when one of our colleagues in the history department, Professor Krause, emailed me yesterday morning to complain about the state of the classroom when he entered it.

"He said he wouldn't have cared if he needed to erase the board a little bit, saying he's also forgotten to clean up before, but his students seemed alarmed by the pentagrams that were not merely drawn on the board but taped to the walls. He looked up the master schedule to see who had the classroom before and found out it was you, and then he contacted me, as your chair. He was concerned about your mental state, for you to post those symbols, or have your students post those symbols, all over the classroom and leave them there. He said it didn't seem to be a 'sound educational practice.'"

Candace sighed. "I agree with him. Marissa, this really is quite bizarre. *What* is going on with you?"

*I became insane, with long intervals of horrible sanity.* Poe's quote came to mind, but thankfully I held my tongue.

"Candace, I don't understand. I didn't *do* that. I drew the symbols on the board to go along with my lesson, and I guess I forgot to erase them." This part was untrue, as I wanted someone to see them, *wanted* to draw out the killer. "I didn't tape any drawings to the walls, though. I don't know why he would say that." I didn't know this man, so he had no axe to grind with me. There was no reason for him to make this up.

Candace brought out her phone, fidgeted with it for a few moments, and handed it to me. "He sent pictures, too," she said. "Look, and tell me that you didn't do this."

Sure enough, there were my drawings from class, but there were also scores of papers taped to the walls, each of which contained a pentacle or pentagram, and most were upside down.

I looked into her eyes. Though I hadn't been 100% truthful with her, I wanted her to read my honesty. "Candace, I *didn't* do this. And how could I? Wouldn't the custodian have come to the classroom that night and cleaned up any mess left behind?"

She shrugged. "I thought of that, as well, but maybe they were afraid a professor had set it up for a class, so they didn't do anything to avoid being punished for interfering with a faculty member's display. Or maybe the custodian forgot to clean the room—that happens from time to time, just as they sometimes forget to unlock a classroom door. I didn't think to ask him if the trash was taken or not. I don't think that Professor Krause was worried about trash, though. He was worried why any professor would *do* this to a classroom. You must admit that these photos are alarming."

"Candace, you have to believe me. I *didn't* do this. Someone else did. Maybe someone wanted me to get in trouble." *The same person threatening me with the notes,* I wanted to add, but I couldn't get into all that.

"Why would someone possibly sneak into a classroom and do that? This campus is traumatized by the death of a student. Do you really think someone would bother with a practical joke right now?" Candace finished her wine and set down her glass. Lowering her voice, even though we were alone, she asked, "Is it possible that you don't remember?"

"No, I didn't do it! I remember everything that happened yesterday! What are you saying, Candace?" I blinked away angry, hurt tears that distorted my vision. I guzzled the rest of my wine just to give myself something to do.

"Marissa, your behavior has been erratic lately," she said. "I stopped by during your office hours a few days ago to see you, and you weren't there. And don't tell me you were in the bathroom, since your door was locked. You're required by contract to make yourself available unless you reschedule and notify secretarial staff. I checked with Margie, and she claimed you didn't email her."

"What? No, I've been to all of my office hours! When did you stop by? I'm positive I didn't skip anything." I replayed my calendar of the last week in my mind to see if there was a conflicting appointment, but my mind drew a blank. My eyes still seemed fuzzy, and I rubbed at them, forgetting that I had eye makeup on that I was probably smearing all over my face. A pain began throbbing on the left side of my head.

Candace's voice grew a tad louder. "There's more. Our student worker, Stephanie, complained that you practically slammed the door in her face when she was coming into the building after you the other day. She said she knows you were probably lost in thought and didn't mean it, but she said you seemed like you didn't look right."

"I don't remember *anything* like that. I always hold doors open for people. It's something I love about working here, how people do that for each other," I mumbled. I liked Stephanie and always said hello when I saw her. I would never intentionally slam the door on her, but it was possible I wasn't paying attention.

"There's *still* more, Marissa. Trust me, I'm not the only person who's concerned about your behavior. And you yourself said you haven't been sleeping well." Candace threaded her fingers together and peered at me over the top of her glasses, her eyebrows arched.

A flash of rage surged through me. "I didn't tape up those signs, and I went to office hours, and maybe I didn't hold open the door, and whatever else anyone said, but it's been a bad couple of weeks, Candace! My student died. And I had to talk to her parents, and meet with homicide detectives, and go to the funeral, and moving here was supposed to make things better for me, not worse!"

I took a few deep breaths, feeling overwhelmed and a little woozy as fatigue overtook me. Leaning back into the cushions, I slowed my voice and added, "You *know* me. You know I'm not a bad person and that I'm not crazy, if that's what you're implying."

I had drunk only the one glass of wine, but it had hit me hard. I started feeling like I was drifting away from this awful conversation even though I needed to finish it and vindicate myself.

Just then, I heard the faint buzz of a text coming in. Not caring if I was being rude at this point with the way she was treating me, I pulled my phone out to read a text from Jake through blurry vision: *Candace is Kai's aunt. You need to get out. You're not safe.*

I closed my eyes and sank into the couch.

# CHAPTER 33

I came to slowly. *Had I fallen asleep? For how long?*
Candace loomed over me, inches away. "Are you awake?"

"What happened?" I asked, suddenly aware of an itch on my scalp. Moving to scratch it, I realized my hands were bound behind my back and that I was lying on my side on the floor of Candace's living room. After shifting my weight onto my shoulder, I propped myself up against the couch. "What the hell is going on? And Kai was your *niece*?"

My mind raced to fill in the gaps. We had been talking about my so-called unstable behavior, I received Jake's text, and then I felt sleepy. The combined feelings of dizziness and nausea made it all hard to process.

Candace stood up from her crouch, ignoring my question. I trailed her with my eyes as she walked into the kitchen and poured herself another glass of wine. She had dimmed the lights from earlier; a single mason jar pendant stayed on. Candace's house had metamorphosed from safe haven to prison, the descended darkness seeming to have fallen over her

"How many times have you come to my house since you moved back, Marissa?" she demanded, walking back to the living room and taking a sip.

"I don't know, like four or five?" This didn't seem like the most important thing to discuss right now. Darting my eyes around the room, I tried to see if someone else had joined us.

"Did you ever look at my house, closely examine it?"

This time *I* ignored *her* question. "Candace, I don't understand what's going on, but I'm not feeling well, and you need to untie me." My heart seemed to pound in my head as bile crawled up my throat. I swallowed it down along with my sense of impending dread. "I have to leave."

"You imbibed such a light dose that I'm surprised how quickly it affected you. It's my own special blend—valerian root, lavender, and chamomile. I thought you'd need a second glass of wine."

Her voice, cold and distant, sounded so different than that of the woman I had known for more than two decades, as if the warmth and friendliness had been removed with a scalpel, leaving only the timbre. "It seems so *strange* to me that you've come here as my guest, that we've been in contact via phone and email all these years, yet you never took the time to see what was lying right in front of you. You never picked up on *any* of it."

I couldn't contain my frustration any longer, even with the new knowledge of who she was. "What are you *talking* about? Yes, I've come here as your guest, and I've always brought wine or something to eat, and complimented you on your beautiful house! Why are you *doing* this to me?"

She didn't look at me and didn't answer—she was staring at her shelving. "We sat here so many times, and you never noticed. And you never asked. Over the years, even before you came to Blackthorn, I listened to you whine about your alcoholic dad and trailer park background, how you couldn't get pregnant, Emma's death and your divorce, all of it. But you never asked me how *I* was doing, Marissa. You never asked me about *my* family or the problems *I* had."

"I'm sorry if I was a bad friend," I whispered, my pulse quickening as I wondered if Candace was breaking down.

Maybe I could talk her out of whatever she was planning. Normal people did *not* drug and tie up their friends, even if those friends were self-centered. I shifted my fingers behind me to see if, by some miracle, my cell phone was on the ground and I could access it, but I didn't feel it anywhere.

"I didn't want to pry. I thought you *liked* being private. You never brought up anything personal—we always talked about work, or literature, or what was going on with me." Saying it aloud made me realize how unbalanced this friendship was, but it didn't excuse whatever the hell she was playing at.

She walked over and picked up one of the picture frames. A sneer darted across her face for a moment and then disappeared without a trace, her expression detached once more.

I squinted in the dim light to make out the details of the photograph: a group of people hugging and smiling at the beach. There were a couple of older people with white hair, a portly middle-aged guy who looked kind of familiar with his arms around the waist of a woman with her head turned so you couldn't see her face, and there was Candace, her blonde bob giving her away. Next to her was another blonde, even leaner and shorter than Candace.

Kai. *My* Kai.

I breathed out a deep sigh. I didn't know how Jake had pieced it together, but here it was. He was right. My tormentor —not that I had told him everything about the threats—had been hiding, like that damned purloined letter, in the most obvious place, as my *friend*, the one person who had seemed to stick by me all those years when others came and went. The betrayal hit me like a punch in the face.

And yet, I had betrayed Kai, and by extension her family, by going along with the coverup.

Candace didn't wait for me to wrap my head around all of my competing emotions. "We went to the beach that summer, all of us: my parents, younger sister, her husband, and her daughter. My *niece*. My single legacy in this world since I never had children and my sister could only have the one. And you took her from us, or at least you didn't tell us what happened. This is what *this*"—she waved her wine glass-holding hand toward me, spilling a few drops on the hardwood floor—"is about, Marissa. I gave you so many opportunities to come clean and tell the truth."

"I didn't hurt Kai," I said, although my guilt brimmed to the surface once more, wanting to overflow. "What happened was an *accident*. Don't do anything stupid, Candace. I'll tell the police, and you, everything I remember about that night, I promise. The detective has already put it together, how you and I are both connected to Kai. He *told* me."

"Your word means nothing to me. You lied before and will do it again. We're not going to the police. We're taking a ride."

After draining her wine, she grabbed me by the arm and yanked me to my feet. "If you scream for help when we go outside, I will plunge this athame into your flesh." She held up an ornate dagger.

"*You* wrote the threatening notes," I said, comprehending despite my grogginess as we walked toward her car. "*You* placed those papers in my classroom."

"There *were* no papers. It's Photoshop. I decided to rattle your cage a bit, is all. There was no student complaint, either, though I *did* hear about what happened in your class. And, yes, I broke into your apartment, but that was before I'd even heard about your silly stunt. Norman is a sweet boy. I never would have hurt him, but I wanted you to know that you were vulnerable. And, the truth is, even after all this time, I wasn't sure what to do about you. I needed something to hold over you in case you told anyone about me drugging and questioning you if I decided to let you go.

"But I've made up my mind. I'm not letting you go. You can disappear, just like my niece did all those years ago. You have no one. Unlike Kai, you don't have people who will miss you."

*She wasn't going to let me go.* I chose to ignore this as well as her heart-wrenching truth about me. I needed to keep her talking, to ask questions of my own. None of this made *sense*.

"But why go through all of this? Why act like I was your friend? Why ask me to apply here? I don't understand." Still foggy with the concoction she'd given me, my brain refused to catch up.

"So many questions, Marissa. I wanted you to come back so you could tell me the truth. That's all. Simple," she answered.

"But what does Kai have to do with the Poppies, or Hadley? And if you wanted me to stop investigating, does that mean you killed Hadley?"

"The Poppies were a vehicle. Hadley was an accident, not to mention none of your concern. You didn't need to stick your nose into it and help the police; you're hardly a moral compass," Candace said, her voice empty. "But don't you understand, yet, who I am?"

"You're Kai's aunt," I said.

"I'm the high priestess, you dumb bitch," she replied, shoving me into the backseat of her car, tightening my restraints, and placing a hood over my head.

LYING sideways on the leather backseat of Candace's Lexus, blinded by the rough fabric covering my face, I had no idea where we were going. Candace wouldn't say, but she told me plenty of other information. After Kai disappeared, Candace's sister and brother-in-law were so grief-stricken that they were practically catatonic, and they put all their faith in God and the police. Candace, meanwhile, wanted to take matters into her own hands, so she left her tenure-track job at a small liberal arts college in Maine for a one-year position as a visiting professor at Blackthorn. She was already a practicing Wiccan by then, having become fascinated with paganism and nature worship as part of her doctoral studies in folklore.

"Before Kai was taken, my craft was all love and light. I celebrated the Wheel of the Year and set positive intentions," she told me. "With my coven in Maine, I danced in the woods and pledged loyalty to the goddess. Afterward, I wanted answers and revenge. I turned to darker arts."

With her spells—or so she claimed—she managed to extend her contract and convert to tenure track at Blackthorn University. She cast out for girls in OKB, especially those of us whom Kai had mentioned by name, to interact with her, either as students in her classes or just in passing.

"When I saw your name, Kai's supposed best friend, on my class list, I knew I was progressing. But, for all my efforts and pushes, you never caved. You never stepped up and did what was right. So I continued my quest, laser-focused on you, the one who had betrayed her the most."

I heard very little traffic, which probably meant we were heading out of town. I had tried interrupting and reasoning with her, but she wouldn't listen—*she* wanted to talk for once, she said.

She told me how she started an affair with a policeman and coerced him into sharing files about Kai's case. She read all the transcripts from the interviews, mine and those of the other girls.

"Several of you said the exact same thing—that Kai must have left when you were sleeping, that she was sleepwalking, which she had done before, as a child, but it didn't add up. No, it didn't!"

Candace lowered and raised her voice, speaking fast at times like she wanted to throw all the words out but then prolonged her syllables. She was all over the place.

"The testimony of you and the other pledges, especially, sounded too rehearsed. Some of the other girls offered up ideas, at least, like that she took off with a secret boyfriend no one knew about, but all of *you* stuck to the sleepwalking story. You didn't even bother to float out any theories on what happened while she was *supposedly* sleepwalking."

I could almost taste the bitterness in Candace's voice, the same voice that had comforted me in times of sorrow and propelled me to get back on my feet when all I wanted was to crawl into bed. I thought she was my true friend, but it was all a charade. All of it. Maybe it was what I deserved, my punishment for lying about Kai.

*We wear the mask that grins and lies.* Paul Laurence Dunbar's words entered my consciousness. Candace had been wearing a mask all this time and was only now exposing her true self.

And she was terrifying.

"When I wasn't getting anywhere, and neither were the cops, I knew my spells weren't powerful enough. I required a coven. That's where the Poppies came into it. Kai had called me and told me things about pledging, details she would never have shared with her parents. I became obsessed with the psychology of it all, that desperate feeling to belong. So I came up with the Poppies, a secret sorority where I hand-picked girls who seemed to need an outlet. I started small, reaching out to three girls in my classes whom I thought were strong leaders and might be open to serving a higher power."

"But did your spells *work*?" I tried not to sound as skeptical as I felt so as not to provoke her—she'd already threatened to make me disappear.

"Of course they did! I wanted to meet Kai's friends, and I did. I cast out for you to come back to Blackthorn, and you arrived, just as I intended." Her voice had become sing-song, and I wondered if she was beginning to unravel or if this was just who she was, the *real* Candace.

It's not that I was close-minded—maybe some people *did* harness powers. But I hadn't come back to Blackthorn because of a spell. I came back since my former life had been messed up and I wanted a fresh start, and there was a job available to which Candace *suggested* I apply. That was all it was, not witchcraft.

And, if I were really being honest with myself, maybe I came back because I had never gotten past what had happened in the woods. I needed to face up to my role in Kai's death.

Candace stayed quiet for several minutes, making me wonder if she was done spilling her secrets, but she began again with the same frantic pace.

"Why would I hide behind a sorority, is that what you want to know? It was intriguing, the secret nature of it. If I posted a flier announcing a witchcraft group, I knew I might not get the kind of girls I wanted, girls who might help me achieve greatness. I worked with my three to help them begin developing their own powers, and the next semester we looked for recruits.

"We agreed to proceed cautiously with the new girls so they wouldn't get scared. The first three weeks of pledging were much like any other Greek life experience—pay your dues, show respect to the sisters. I wasn't involved with any of that. The weak ones would drop before the leaders introduced elements of the craft, slowly, when the pledges were already invested in becoming one of the Poppies.

"Once we tattooed the pentacle on them, however, they couldn't quit—the dark lord would not allow it. I would lead the rituals, wearing a mask to protect my privacy. Only the original three ever knew who I was. We all enhanced our powers, together, some girls sticking to simple good luck charms, others becoming more advanced."

As she spoke, taking me through her warped plan, I struggled to piece these two versions of Candace together: the academic who published research and presented at conferences with this unhinged woman who had kidnapped me and thought she had magical powers.

It didn't add up, but I chose my next words carefully to keep her talking. "But why kill Hadley?" I asked. "What did you gain from Hadley's death?"

"Hadley was a tragic accident," Candace replied, echoing the words that had once been uttered about her niece. "She was pregnant, and the coven performed a spell on her to rid her of the unwanted fetus while using the opportunity to increase our powers with the sacrifice. She understood the risk of the procedure. She would have become a powerful witch." Candace said these last few words with reverence as if she were truly regretful for what happened.

But being sorry wasn't enough. Fury boiled in my fingertips and shot up my arms, but I still couldn't loosen my bindings. "You gave her roofies and performed an unsafe abortion on her. She bled out and *died*, and you left her in the woods, and who knows what you did to the fetus. That's not a spell, Candace! It was a botched medical procedure. She could have gone to Planned Parenthood and been fine. This is on *you*. And now you've brought all these girls into it."

"The drugs were for the pain. I would have preferred a more natural concoction, but Hadley desired something stronger. We completed our ritual with the fetus so Hadley's sacrifice would matter. We heightened our powers. And don't act superior, Marissa, it's not a good look on you. Besides, we're here."

From my prone position in the backseat, I felt the car brake and then stop. Candace slammed her door, opened mine, and yanked me to a standing position.

As the cold air tore through my clothing, I listened for clues as to where we were, but all I could hear was the mournful sigh of the wind.

"The cops are onto you, Candace. Detective Ruiz texted me—he didn't think I was safe with you. He's coming after you. You should turn yourself in before things get even worse."

"Shh. Be a good girl and *do* shut the fuck up for once in your miserable life," she responded.

I was alone with a crazy woman, one without medical training who had stood by and not called for help as a young woman bled to death in front of her. I was alone with a lunatic hell-bent on revenge against me.

# CHAPTER 34

"W here are we? What are we doing here?" I asked as Candace guided me over the rocky terrain.

"We're at Water's Edge, Marissa, and I'm bringing you for a ritual. The Poppies and I will perform a truth-telling spell so you finally reveal what happened to Kai," Candace said, clutching my arm tighter.

"You don't need to go through all of that. I'll *tell* you. I told you that we can go to the police."

"No police. It's too late for that. We'll do things my way now."

*Police.*

Jake thought Candace was dangerous since she was Kai's aunt, which meant he knew more than he had told me about Kai. He must've discovered that I was hiding something if he thought I was at risk. But I couldn't worry about that part right now, what Jake knew about my past. I was more concerned about his understanding of the present. Had he figured out that Candace was behind Hadley's death? He was supposed to come to my apartment at ten p.m., but he wouldn't have waited around for that if he thought my life was in jeopardy. I had no idea how long I'd been passed out from the herbal cocktail—potion?—she'd slipped into my wine. But where *was* he?

He knew who Candace was, and I said I was having a drink with her, so wouldn't he have gone to her house and seen my car? I tried to remember if it was still in the driveway when we left; she might have hidden it in her garage. And she also might have texted Jake from my phone and told him everything was fine.

A smart, devious woman, Candace must have thought long and hard about what she was doing. Then again, her behavior, even her speech and mannerisms, had become unpredictable. Maybe she forgot a detail somewhere, and Jake would find us here and bring Candace to justice.

I didn't want to think about the alternative. Back at her house, she said she was no longer worried about me telling on her.

No, she didn't want to kill me. She *couldn't*. Could she? Hadley was gone, but it was unintentional. Candace wasn't a real murderer, not exactly.

We kept walking, and I wondered where she was taking me. It would be easy enough to push me off a cliff, to untie me at the bottom and make it appear accidental. I imagined her being interviewed about my death, and she'd tell Jake how my behavior had become strange, how I was messing up and acting irresponsibly. She'd tell Jake I was obsessed with Hadley's death, and Jake might believe it. He'd seen proof *himself*, even warning me that I should back off and move on.

But that text he sent. He smelled danger, had made connections despite how both Candace and I had tried to keep them hidden.

Poor Hadley. In all of this, she was an innocent, friendless girl who wanted to belong, a girl whose life was ripped away from her all because she was unlucky enough to be marked as someone who might increase Candace's so-called powers. When Hadley kept that horseshoe necklace and agreed to pledge, she changed the path of her fate. I wondered if there were any other casualties over the years Candace had been grooming students into witches.

"What happened to Audrey Quarto? Did she die during a ritual, too?" I asked after a period of quiet, wanting to get her talking so I could keep track of her thoughts.

"Audrey? No, she quit pledging before I even met her. Audrey was a frivolous girl without the discipline for the craft. She went into a mental institution, and then she fled, relocating to North Dakota. One of the Poppies tracked her down, but there was no need to punish her. She didn't matter to us. She knew nothing," Candace said. "But *you* matter, Marissa. You matter quite a bit. The girls and I have a special evening planned for you."

As soon as she said it, I heard chanting off in the distance, and I could see just enough through my hood to tell that a raging bonfire was burning. We were approaching the site of the ritual. The closer we walked to whatever this was, the faster my pulse raced.

There I was, back in those woods. Had I ever really *left*? Maybe the price I had to pay for Kai's death, my pound of flesh, was to be killed and abandoned in another unmarked grave. Who would mourn me if I died tonight? Would it provide Candace with the closure she craved? Like Kai, would Water's Edge be my final resting place?

I couldn't give up, even if it were hopeless. "Candace, *think* about what you're doing. Hadley's already dead. You've involved all these girls, and now you want to hurt *me*. These girls will have to carry this with them for the rest of their lives. Don't do this, please."

"Shh. We're almost there. I need to put on my mask for the ceremony."

We kept walking, tramping over dead leaves, maybe traversing some of the same ground I had covered the previous night. I couldn't tell.

The chanting came to an abrupt halt as we reached the gathering.

"My witches, my Poppies, your high priestess has arrived," Candace said, her voice muffled from whatever she had placed over her face. I wondered if any of the girls were students in her classes. Wouldn't they recognize her voice?

"Greetings, High Priestess. We welcome you in our worship," voices intoned together, a frightful Greek chorus. I couldn't make out anything from beneath my hood except for the blaze of the fire, so I didn't know how many girls there were.

"Tonight we will perform the Ritual of Truth. Tonight I bring you a liar. She has hidden the facts from the police about what happened to an innocent girl. Tonight we will make her tell, and our powers will grow, in witches and sisterhood."

Sisterhood? Rituals? This reminded me of my own pledging experience, but at least no one had *intended* to cause harm. The Cliff of Life Ritual had been irresponsible since we were bordering on hypothermia and somewhat intoxicated, but it was a tradition to bind us through sisterhood.

Is that what these girls thought now, as I stood before them, that this was harmless? How could they think that after what had happened to Hadley, one of their own? Why were they so *calm*?

Candace pushed me to the ground, where I tumbled in a heap, my bound hands rendering me unable to reach out and break my fall.

"A liar must tell the truth or pay for her sins. You are here now, before this circle, to tell your part in Kai's disappearance. With these words and these herbs, we bind you in a truth spell."

The fire crackled and flamed hotter as something I couldn't see was thrown in.

"A liar must tell the truth or pay for her sins," the voices repeated around me.

"With a lock of your hair we bind you to tell the truth," Candace said. Stooping over me, she lifted part of my hood and pulled my hair, hacking some off and throwing it into the fire. The acrid smell infiltrated my nostrils, making my eyes water as my scalp burned from pain.

"Behold this liar!" Candace said, pulling off my hood.

I blinked, my eyes straining to adjust. From the light of the fire, I could see about nine cloaked figures, standing in a semi-circle, all of them with hoods drawn low over their faces. Candace, also cloaked but wearing some kind of a goat mask, held her dagger in one hand, leaning over me.

With my heart in my throat, I prepared for what would come next: chanting, bloodletting, whatever it was. Petrified, my body rigid with cold and fear, I waited for my fate.

But then the spell broke.

"Oh my God! Dr. Owens? Is that you? Are you okay?" one of the witches said.

I didn't recognize the voice, but I realized that this was my shot—appealing to their humanity. No adult had been there on Hell Night when we made our decision all those years ago. As much as we understood that our futures were on the line, we didn't have the foresight to see how damaging the path we took would be to ourselves as well as others, Kai's family in particular. Going along with the group back then led me to this very bonfire.

If only I could reverse time and give myself advice now that I was older and wiser. I couldn't, but I had an opportunity to help these girls make a better choice, one that could save my skin, as well. I took a deep breath, knowing that the words I uttered could be my last.

"No, I'm not okay. I'm terrified. I don't know how far she's willing to go—she told me I might disappear. She wants to punish me for a bad decision I made in college, one I've regretted my whole life."

My petition came out weak and tremulous, but I summoned my strength and continued. "Girls, don't *do* this. You'll carry it with you for the rest of your lives. I've carried my secret, and it's brought me here. Help me, please."

Candace grabbed me by the hair. "Don't listen to this liar. She must pay for her sins."

"Stop! This is my professor!" The witch who had spoken pulled off her hood and rushed to my side. It was Carly, a girl in my Poe class. She'd been a stellar student at the beginning of the semester, but her work ethic had fallen off. Now it made sense—she'd dabbled in a world even darker than Poe's.

Carly began crying, her words garbled with sobs. "It was fun at first, but it got so out of hand, and then Hadley died and we couldn't tell anyone what happened, and I *can't do this anymore*. I told her about the pentacles in class, only because it connected with our craft. But I didn't know she was *after* you." She started fumbling with the ties around my wrists, trying to loosen them, but her hands shook too much to get a grip on the rope.

"As your high priestess, I *forbid* you to untie her. She is a liar who must atone for her sins. Bringing her to justice will increase our powers," Candace said, her words flat, as if her power over the girls was draining.

One of the other witches stepped forward. "What about all of *us*? Shouldn't we be brought to justice? I don't know what *this* lady did, but look what *we* did! Hadley is *dead*, and we let it happen! I can't eat, I can't sleep, all I can think about is that we left Hadley in these woods and went about our lives!"

She ripped off her hood, revealing a face unknown to me

and a wild mass of dark hair, but the firelight revealed the anguish in her wide-eyed expression and contorted mouth. She rushed to my side and joined Carly in freeing me.

I watched as two more stepped forward and removed their hoods. They no longer looked like witches; they looked like scared college girls.

Candace held up her dagger. "Stop, I command you, or the dark lord will smite you with his wrath!"

"No. This has gone too far, and it needs to stop now so nothing else bad happens," another witch said, declaring the words I should have been brave enough to say that night twenty-four years earlier. "Grab her. Tie her up." The nameless young woman pointed, and the circle began closing in around Candace.

Rubbing my chafed wrists, I tried to step up into some kind of authoritarian role. "Careful! She could hurt you!" I lunged forward, breaking their circle, only to see Candace stretch out both arms before letting the dagger fall. Defeated, she crumpled to a heap on the ground and began emitting low, animal-like sounds that gave me goosebumps for the raw pain and fear they contained.

I watched mutely as one of the girls used the discarded rope to tie Candace's hands behind her back.

"We'll help keep her here, Dr. Owens," Carly told me. "We need to call the cops."

---

AFTER AN INTERMINABLE WAIT, I heard it, the disembodied voice from the bullhorn. "Step away from the fire. All of you. Get down on your knees and put your hands up."

I joined the others, dragging myself up to my knees and raising my arms. I was more than just a victim; Candace was correct that I had to account for my own sins. As I peered into the darkness, the shapes of several police officers crept out like mist from the trees. When they came closer, illuminated by the fire, I saw Welch and others I didn't recognize.

And Jake. There was Jake, come to set matters right, whatever that meant for me.

# CHAPTER 35

"Candace Cabrera, you are under arrest for suspicion of manslaughter in the death of Hadley Parker and the kidnapping of Marissa Owens."

The scene that unfurled in front of me was so surreal that I could barely comprehend what was happening. Welch untied the witches' sloppy rope bindings on Candace's arms and replaced them with handcuffs, but only after removing her mask. She looked like what she was: not any sort of high priestess or well-published academic, just a manic woman approaching old age, thrashing, hissing, and yelling about the dark lord as Welch read her the Miranda rights.

The witches, the ones who hadn't fled after I was freed, weren't handcuffed or placed under arrest, but they were told that they had the right to legal counsel. Some of the girls were clutching themselves or each other and crying, while others stared straight ahead, resigned to accept the consequences of their actions.

Not knowing what to do, and still pulsing with fear, I stayed on my knees as Jake came over.

"Marissa, come on, get up. It's over now," he said, his voice strained with exhaustion. As near as he was, he didn't reach out to touch or embrace me. I couldn't help but read into that.

*What* part *is over*? I wondered. I didn't know what all the police had discovered, and I had only shared the minimum when I called from Carly's phone, wanting them to hurry up. They must have figured out enough to arrest Candace.

"I think I need to come with you for questioning," I said, getting up anyway, my limbs stiff with my confinement, my clothes covered with dirt and debris. This was *not* the night I had planned when I texted him earlier in the day.

"Careful," he said, steadying me as I stumbled. "And, yes, you *do* need to come in. But if what I saw gives me any clue what you've been through tonight, I think you might need to breathe first. We can wait until morning. It's almost midnight."

*The witching hour*, I thought.

"I think I've waited long enough to tell the truth," I said. "It's time."

I couldn't read his expression in the light of the diminishing fire, which was already being put out by one of the officers, but he nodded and took my arm, more like a detective than a lover. "I should recuse myself due to the nature of our, uh, relationship," he said.

"No. It needs to be you. I would like for you to be there, too, along with someone else if needed." As much as part of me didn't want Jake to know about my past, whatever he hadn't already figured out for himself, the rest of me did. If this relationship—his word, not mine—had any future, he deserved to know who I was, darkness and all.

He looked at me hard then, his features shadowed, but I could read the disappointment and sadness in his eyes. "I don't know everything, not yet, but I have my guesses. I'm hoping you can fill me in back at the station."

*Back at the station.* I was a suspect now.

---

I RODE in the back of the unmarked police car with Jake and Welch.

"You're not under arrest, Dr. Owens," Welch told me as he opened up the door. "But we *will* need your statement."

"State*ments*," Jake corrected. "What happened tonight as well as what happened back then." They were the only words he uttered during the whole ride, despite the persistent drone of Welch's voice as he talked about nothing that had to do with anything.

I also stayed quiet in the backseat and closed my eyes, which felt like two hot coals in my head. As much as I wasn't a huge fan of Welch, I was grateful for his presence in the car. I don't know if I could have tolerated the tension if I were alone with Jake.

Jake, who could have been sleeping in my bed at that moment if the night had gone differently, seemed as far away and unreachable as ever.

---

STARING at the Styrofoam cup of bitter coffee in front of me back at the station, noticing the faint hum of the fluorescent lights, I avoided Jake's eyes.

*Out with it.* Phoebe already knew I was planning to tell, which made it easier. She'd asked me to give her a few days, but I didn't have a choice at this point.

"Dr. Owens, I want to restate that you are *not* under arrest, but you have the right to an attorney before you provide your statement. Also, for the purpose of the recording, the witness asked for Detective Ruiz to be present while she makes her statement despite the nature of their relationship, one which did not start until after the witness was dismissed as a suspect in the death of Hadley Parker. I will be in charge of conducting the questioning."

Although I had thought of him as gruff in my previous meetings, Welch had treated me kindly, even fetching the coffee before leading me into the interrogation room, a bland space that housed some spindly chairs and a lopsided table.

I nodded, showing I understood. "I do not want an attorney at this time," I said, words an attorney was sure to chastise me for later.

"Okay then. Please tell us what occurred tonight, how you came to be tied up in front of the bonfire in the woods."

"I want to tell how it all started, first," I began. "It all goes back to October 16, 1998. That was the night that my best friend, Kai McDougall, fell off a cliff and died. And then we hid her body."

# BLACKTHORN GAZETTE

***Police: Missing girl's remains found at Water's Edge twenty-four years after disappearance***
*by Reggie Hawthorne*

Posted October 28, 2022 / 11:15 AM

Blackthorn, Pa. – Human remains were discovered at Water's Edge State Park this morning after suspect Phoebe Klein led detectives to the makeshift burial site. The remains have been identified by authorities as Kai McDougall, a woman missing since 1998.

As first reported by the *Blackthorn Gazette's* Marcia Benedict on October 19, 1998, the 19-year-old Blackthorn University sophomore disappeared from the Omega Kappa Beta sorority house on East Market Street sometime after 11 p.m. on the night of October 16 and before 7 a.m. on the morning of October 17.

McDougall and four other students were pledges of the OKB sorority, a local Greek organization that no longer holds a chapter at BU. Witnesses, including OKB president Danielle Flowers, claimed that McDougall was present during the sorority function of the night before but was gone when the sorority sisters woke the pledges for the initiation ceremony the next morning.

In interviews with the *Blackthorn Gazette*, McDougall's four pledge sisters, all of whom spent the night at the sorority house, revealed no knowledge of McDougall's whereabouts. In follow-up interviews with the sorority sisters, victim's family members, school officials, classmates, and residents of Blackthorn, speculation about what happened to McDougall included theories ranging from human trafficking to alien abduction.

The lead investigating officer at the time, Detective Ross Schumacher, was quoted as saying, "The girls are not telling all of the facts." But the police failed to uncover additional evidence, and the case went cold despite the efforts of McDougall's family members to keep the investigation open.

According to authorities, former OKB sorority sister Phoebe Klein, 45, confessed on Thursday morning that she had witnessed McDougall falling off a cliff. She and three other sisters had taken the five pledges to Water's Edge for a sorority ritual that went against Blackthorn University rules at the time and would be illegal today under hazing laws. Klein stated that she and the other suspects were worried about getting in trouble and colluded to conceal McDougall's death and hide the body. Klein maintains that the rest of the sorority did not know that she and the others left the house together that night.

"We just want to bring her home now," the victim's mother, Linda McDougall, 68, of Bangor, Maine, said. "If only her friends had told us what really happened, it would have saved us so much grief over the years."

As reported by the coroner's office, an examination of McDougall's remains indicates the cause of death is consistent with injuries from a fall.

Authorities said they do not suspect foul play, but multiple crimes were committed by the members and pledges of the sorority. Charges are pending on Klein and five other suspects who were present at Water's Edge that night. Two additional women who were there died before today's discovery.

---

The first snowflakes of the season descend from the sky as I gaze out the window from my desk. This is my final batch of papers for the semester—I proctored my last exam today. The thought of freedom from the grind fills my heart with joy. Placing my turquoise pen down, I sip coffee from my Starbucks Paris mug and revel in the beauty of nature and the promise that life will go on.

*Paris.* I'd like to go back someday.

As I await my arraignment, I've had plenty of time to think about the choices I've made in my life. There is no single regret bigger than going along with the agreement to hide Kai's death. Coming forward doesn't make it right, but now Kai's family finally has closure.

My attorney doesn't think my case will go to trial or that I'll serve prison time. She thinks I'll get off with a fine and community service. While no one was arrested, to my knowledge, all six of us who are living have been charged with criminal complaints. My charges are concealing a body and obstruction of justice, which I imagine are the same for everyone else, but I can't find definitive answers online.

I don't know if Phoebe and the others received additional charges for hazing—the laws were different back then, before the rash of deaths across the country that sparked change. It seems unlikely that a crime committed prior to the creation of those laws would result in prosecution today. I haven't spoken to any of the others and don't know how they're handling the strain. There's no need to rekindle relationships with any of them. That chapter of my life is closed, and it's time to move past it.

I've also learned that Candace has resigned from Blackthorn University, probably to avoid being fired. She admitted what she did to Hadley and what she planned to do to me. The press has had a field day with the sensational elements of both cases, Kai's and Hadley's. I've turned down all requests for interviews, having been told I can't speak about the details until everything is settled in court.

I allow myself fifteen minutes a day to search for new developments online. My therapist says that it's healthy to be curious, but she advises exercising caution so as not to become obsessed. Seeing my name on the front page of the local newspaper has been alarming, but mine has been more of a footnote than the main attraction. Rumors swarmed through the campus like locusts about what had happened, and my students behaved strangely around me for a few days, but they soon learned that the professor who had been kidnapped and might have been sacrificed at a bonfire, the same professor who had her own shocking secret, still required them to write papers and participate in class.

Having a therapist is new to me. My lawyer recommended it, saying it would look good to the judge, but I've found it helpful in processing the various traumas of my life. I'm moving forward, one day at a time.

Based on what I've heard and read in the paper, the Poppies/witches all face criminal charges but haven't been expelled. The fact that a faculty member led them astray was a mitigating factor, as was my plea to the president of the university himself, Andrew Lattimore, who turns out to be a pretty decent and caring guy. I know how one fatal decision can disrupt someone's life, and the girls weren't the ones who caused Hadley's death. I explained all of that to him in the hopes that the girls could learn and grow from the experience rather than allowing it to eat them up. I suggested that the university require both mandatory counseling and community service as probationary conditions for remaining enrolled.

I was upfront and honest with President Lattimore about my own pending charges, as well, explaining that I understood if he didn't want me to teach during the spring semester even though I was contracted to do so. He asked me to stay, saying that my involvement had helped solve Hadley's case, and we would reevaluate future employment after my arraignment, depending on the outcome. We were already down a faculty member in the English Department, and he knows me to be a fierce student advocate, he said.

So, for now, I'll remain at Blackthorn, and I'll find something else to do if there's no place for me here next year. A few of my colleagues teach at the local women's prison part-time, and that might be an area to explore.

My phone buzzes with an incoming text.

It's Jake, asking what time I want to meet him for dinner. Smiling, I respond.

Things were difficult for us for a while. We had to negotiate where we stood with each other after everything that happened, especially with my new criminal charges and the optics of him dating me. It turned out he had already suspected that I knew more than I had disclosed to the police about Kai's disappearance, even before he found out about Candace's connection to Kai.

Like Candace, he had spent some time going through the

old transcripts, but his focus had been on Hadley rather than Kai, and he hoped he was wrong about his instincts. He wasn't, but he told me he was proud of me for coming forward, finally, and we had a whole conversation about trust to a depth I'd never reached in my marriage to David. We agreed that we would not discuss police matters in either of the cases before the trials so as not to obfuscate our blossoming relationship.

We also decided on no more sleepovers until we got to know each other better, but that rule didn't last long.

For Christmas, he wants me to meet his family. I'm nervous, of course, but excited that we're taking this next step. Regarding *my* family members, my therapist has suggested that I make more of an effort to connect. I'm ready to try, and maybe someday I'll get to introduce Jake to them.

With so much to lose, Jake asked me why I decided to tell the truth now, after all these years.

I did it for Kai, whose body was finally put to rest, whose family needed the answers they sought all this time.

I did it for Hadley, whose death forced me to face what had happened in the past and take accountability for it.

I did it for Emma, my sweet girl who never got to live but would always remain in my heart. As her mother, as *a* mother, I could no longer allow someone's child's fate to go unknown.

I did it for myself, to finally push past the darkness, past the shadows, and head to a future.

The snow grows heavier, blanketing the street and trees with crystalline sparkle, renewing what had been simply slush and grime.

# Acknowledgments

Without the encouragement of a number of people, this book would remain unwritten. I am first and foremost grateful to my family: my husband, Simon, who has always supported me as I pursued my goals; my parents, John and Niki, who instilled a love of literature and a strong work ethic in me; my daughter, Serena, who helped guide me to a major plot decision; and my siblings, Sarah, Sian, Eleanore, and Garth—the first person to read the completed draft of this novel—who have cheered me on along the way. And, while not *technically* family, my best friend, Beth Peterson, deserves a special shout-out for helping me remember aspects of college life in the late nineties.

I have always dreamt of becoming a published novelist, but this only became a reality after finding a writing community. The Maslow Family Graduate Program in Creative Writing at Wilkes University provided me with the tools I needed to hone my craft and learn the business. I am particularly thankful for my mentor, J. Michael Lennon, who helped me reduce overwriting, pushed me to avoid clichés, and pointed out plot holes. Also, I am beyond appreciative of my wonderful cohort members in the program who became close friends as we all settled into our writer identities, struggling and thriving together.

Finally, I am forever indebted to the Wicked House Publishing team for taking a chance on me.

# ABOUT THE AUTHOR

Cassandra O'Sullivan Sachar is a writer and associate English professor in Pennsylvania who teaches creative writing and composition classes. A career educator, she previously worked as an English teacher in Delaware public schools. She holds a Doctorate of Education with a Literacy Specialization from the University of Delaware and an MFA in Creative Writing with a focus on horror fiction from Wilkes University. She has traveled to more than fifty countries but also loves being at home with her husband, rescue dog, and a reasonable number of cats.

Visit her website at cassandraosullivansachar.com.
Photo credit: Michael Bruno. mbrunophoto.com

Printed in Great Britain
by Amazon